ADVANCE PRAISE

"This book will equip white educators for their job. If our educators had this outstanding racial literacy toolkit, it would have defogged the racial lies we grew up with and urged us all to reconsider our responsibilities toward each other. It would have altered the trajectory of our time in US K–12 schools."

—**Winona Guo and Priya Vulchi,** cofounders of CHOOSE and authors of *Tell Me Who You Are*

"What readers find when they open *Learning and Teaching While White* is a path to becoming a racially aware white educator. The work may be introspectively challenging, but readers will leave personally and professionally fulfilled. This is not a book, it is a critical, personal exploration of self and system that the authors carefully scaffold to enhance the skill of white educators, both as teachers and as humans."

—**Dr. Eddie Moore Jr.,** Founder, The White Privilege Conference

"Yes! A nuanced and accessible resource for white teachers who have consistently asked, 'What do I do?' This excellent resource answers that question, from two highly experienced white teachers who have been engaged in the work of antiracist practice for decades. This is an essential guidebook that needs to be on every white teacher's shelf."

—**Robin DiAngelo,** author of *White Fragility* and *Nice Racism*

"*Learning and Teaching While White* is the book educators need right now. As reactionary forces seek to stifle equity efforts in schools and intimidate teachers from discussing race, Jenna Chandler-Ward and Elizabeth Denevi have provided an indispensable and practical guide for teachers who know the importance of this work but are uncertain of how to do it. A must-read for all who care about racial equity, the creation of white antiracist solidarity, and the future of America."

—**Tim Wise,** antiracist educator, author of *White Like Me: Reflections on Race From A Privileged Son*

LEARNING
AND TEACHING
WHILE WHITE

Norton Series on Equity and Social Justice in Education
Cheryl E. Matias and Paul C. Gorski, series editors

Norton's Equity and Social Justice in Education series is a publishing home for books that apply critical and transformative equity and social justice theories to the work of on-the-ground educators. Books in the series describe meaningful solutions to the racism, white supremacy, economic injustice, sexism, hetero-sexism, transphobia, ableism, neoliberalism, and other oppressive conditions that pervade schools and school districts.

Learning and Teaching While White
Jenna Chandler-Ward and Elizabeth Denevi

Ableism in Education
Gillian Parekh

Public School Equity
Manya C. Whitaker

Social Studies for a Better World
Noreen Naseem Rodríguez and Katy Swalwell

Equity-Centered Trauma-Informed Education
Alex Shevrin Venet

NORTON BOOKS IN EDUCATION

LEARNING AND TEACHING WHILE WHITE

ANTIRACIST STRATEGIES FOR SCHOOL COMMUNITIES

JENNA CHANDLER-WARD AND ELIZABETH DENEVI

FOREWORD BY HOWARD C. STEVENSON

W. W. NORTON & COMPANY

Independent Publishers Since 1923

Art by Lisa Congdon

For information about permission to reproduce selections from this book, write to Permissions, W. W. Norton & Company, Inc., 500 Fifth Avenue, New York, NY 10110

For information about special discounts for bulk purchases, please contact W. W. Norton Special Sales at specialsales@wwnorton.com or 800-233-4830

Manufacturing by Lake Book Manufacturing
Production manager: Katelyn MacKenzie

ISBN: 978-1-324-01674-8

W. W. Norton & Company, Inc., 500 Fifth Avenue, New York, N.Y. 10110
www.wwnorton.com

W. W. Norton & Company Ltd., 15 Carlisle Street, London W1D 3BS

1 2 3 4 5 6 7 8 9 0

To our students:
thank you for all you have taught us.

CONTENTS

FOREWORD

Have you ever had a social injustice situation that called for you to speak up, one that Martin Luther King might describe as your "drum major for justice" moment? But you found yourself so overwhelmed that instead of speaking up, you tripped up and fell? If you've had this moment, did you question your resolve or courage? Did you doubt if you might ever link your social justice talk with your behavior and *be* that "drum major"? In this book, Jenna Chandler-Ward and Elizabeth Denevi have an answer for these and other powerful questions. The call for clarity on how race and racism matter in our society has been loud in these first two decades of the twenty-first century—almost as loud as the attempts to block the teaching of the history of racism in public and private schooling. Whether we consider how race matters in our schools or in our courtrooms, or in the public thoroughfares that we traverse daily, the politics and hostilities of race and racism have become stark. In their book, Jenna Chandler-Ward and Elizabeth Denevi teach us to stop and look at how these politics are undermining the very basic goals of education: curiosity, learning, and depth of knowledge. The authors help us understand that while these racial politics are not new, they disrupt children's depth of knowledge of the world's past and present, and that could undermine the future.

Chandler-Ward and Denevi argue that without clarity on this country's love affair with racial hierarchy, as well as its potential for racial change, we won't be able to provide a just education for any child, regardless of their race. They issue a plea to understand that the fight for social justice in education is about humanity, forgiveness, and accountability. They call out white people, educators, and justice warriors to pay attention, take notes, and become honest advocates against these efforts by adopting antiracist coping strategies in thought, word, and deed. Not an easy task, but not impossible either. Given the resistance against honesty about racism, they focus on teaching. They focus on the thorny dilemmas that educators must face daily with students of color, who cry out often that what they are learning is unfair to them.   So how does a teacher manage when their own students are calling them out to change the racism in their classroom? Chandler-Ward and Denevi interrogate and illuminate what these racial politics mean for white people and specifically for white teachers. The work of this book is not simply about the rationales behind the systemic nature of racism in education, but the cognitive dissonance that white teachers struggle daily to deny, admit, and ameliorate in the classroom. These racial politics are proximal. The importance of this clarity is no small matter, as racial tensions rise and as legislation to eradicate discussions about race and white privilege from K–12 education rages on across the country. These policies filter down to the classroom, to the relationships, and to the children. What Chandler-Ward and Denevi want to do is to prepare educators for those racially stressful moments.

Beyond clarity, the authors advocate for courage. They want white people to come to a reckoning. This reckoning involves trying to engage—not avoiding—the obvious tensions, factions, and examples of racial dishonesty, avoidance, denial, and privilege.

Chandler-Ward and Denevi start by acknowledging the burden that People of Color have endured by bearing their souls in the service of teaching the world about racial dehumanization, without a meaningful humane response. They acknowledge that if change is going to happen, white people must hold themselves accountable, develop the courage to be challenged, and scale up their competencies to be able to safely navigate racially stressful encounters. That said, they don't recommend or advocate for change without strategy, compassion, or instruction.

Many racial journeys in our country's history have called for conversation between racial groups to come to consensus and reach common goals. While this remains the hallmark of racial progress in this country's legacy, Chandler-Ward and Denevi are suggesting we need more than talk. Socially-just education requires actions louder than words for every classroom, every child, every day.

The authors don't hide the challenges for the audience of white educators to face the truth of their role in racial dehumanization, but they also don't dehumanize educators. What I find refreshing in this work is that Chandler-Ward and Denevi provide roadmaps, definitions, self-reflections, and years of classroom and school experiences to help the reader struggle and rise from that struggle. They provide lampposts when the journey toward social justice gets dark. By being both brutally honest, confessional, and self-reflective about their thoughts and feelings during their difficult moments, the reader can project their fears and identify with strategies to meet those fears head on. To give direct and supportive feedback about the detriment of one's blindness to the awful power of white supremacy (whether the "S" is little or big) in one's teaching of children is a gift. But, to demonstrate steps to hold oneself accountable for that power and that blindness while recognizing redemptive potential in each of us is as humane an expectation as we have in the proximal war against racism. Chandler-Ward and Denevi provide this honesty, accountability, and hope by defining the confusing terms, conditions, and history of how racism embraces the cloak of whiteness and shows up in classroom lessons. They help teachers realize that without attention to anti-racism approaches, they will find their current practices far removed from the earlier reasons of social justice that, dare I say, "drove" them into this much-maligned profession. The stories, practical guidance, and classroom exercises offer so many opportunities for teachers to grow and be agentic, instead of passive, when a social injustice shows up. I look forward to the excitement of building a corps of white teachers who are unafraid to speak truth to power against forces that would rather bury their racial heads into the ground. If you read this book, I suggest you not only ready yourself to be emotionally challenged, even overwhelmed. But if you apply the strategies here as thoroughly as if someone's life depended on it, instead of making excuses, be prepared to engage your next "drum major for justice" trial with much more courage. I doubt you will find your actions inert the next time around.

Howard C. Stevenson, PhD
Constance E. Clayton Professor of Urban Education and Africana Studies
Director, Racial Empowerment Collaborative
University of Pennsylvania
Human Development and Quantitative Methods Division
Graduate School of Education

ACKNOWLEDGMENTS

Our gratitude to our editorial team for their help in developing the manuscript: Paul Gorski, Cheryl Matias, and Carol Collins. To Howard Stevenson for your research, mentorship, and support. Special thank you to our friend and colleague Lisa Congdon for the beautiful cover art. To our early readers Dara Carol and Suzanne Caruso, who described to us the book they wanted to read, and to our later readers, Lori Cohen, Liza Gleason, Anika Nailah, Julia Spiegelman, Malika Carter, Christine Saxman, and Rebecca Watson for their thoughtful feedback. This project could not have been completed without the guidance of our inspirational coach, Katy Dion.

From Teaching While White, we want to thank our advisory committee: Daniel Harris, Claudia Foxtree, Kelly Wickham-Hurst, Dr. Liza Talusan, and Jorge Zaballos. We also have an amazing editorial and production team who support our work to reach as many educators as we can: Michael Brosnan, Wendy Kelly, Jannah Tate, Kate Ellis, Stephen Smith, and Lyra Smith.

Our work is developed via collaboration with many brilliant antiracist educators, and we are inspired by their solidarity and support: Eddie Moore, Jr., Peggy McIntosh, Emily Style, Jennifer Bryan, Kim Parker, Afrika Afeni-Mills, Tim Wise, Rasheda Carroll, Joel Baum, and Ryan Virden. We would like to thank Debby Irving, Jackie Battelora, Christine Saxman, Ali Michael, Shelly Tochluk, Kathy Obear, and Robin DiAngelo for synchronizing flashes of light to increase the brightness of the beam.

We want to thank Yocelin Gonazalez, Alethea Dunham-Carson and the entire Multicultural Teaching Institute (MTI) family for their tireless pursuit of making sure every student feels heard, seen, protected, and treated fairly. MTI has been the home that we always go back to. To the Equity Exchange for all of the beauty, insight, and community that is a lifeline for so many educators.

To our S.T.A.R. students: Maggie Monaghan, Natalie Olivares, Greta Prop, Audrey Prop, and Lily Snyder, thank you for your energy, insight, and work to engage the next generation of antiracist activists.

From Elizabeth:

I've been fortunate to have colleagues who have become family. Thank you to Mariama Richards and Brandi Lawrence for always being there for me and this work to make our students whole. To my two beautiful kids who have always inspired my work and who supported my writing process in a thousand small and big ways. To Jenna Chandler-Ward, who is always willing to run off a cliff with me, thank you for your trust and friendship. And to the first person who told me that I had a part to play in dismantling racism, my love and gratitude to my husband, Randolph Carter. Without him, this project would not have been possible.

From Jenna:

I cannot separate the work I do from the inspiration, guidance, and friendship I have received from Alison Graham, Rosetta Lee, Justin McLean, and Destiny Polk. I hope to give back a fraction of what you have given me. Thank you to Randolph Carter and East Ed for giving me a home, endless support, and encouragement. To Elizabeth Denevi; your mentorship and ride-or-die friendship has taught me what brave love looks like.

I owe my passion to my parents, Connie and David. I hope their spirit is tangible in all that I do, and to the Chandler family that gives me the stable platform to jump from. My well-being springs from the support, feeding, and love that I am so fortunate to receive from Adam Haslett, Courtney Jackson, Andrew Janjigian, Melissa Rivard, and William Yepes. Kenneth Lawrence, thank you for celebrating every small victory, making sure I have what I need, and pushing me to remember what I know when I forget.

My unending love and gratitude to my children, Harper and Henry, who have always supported my work even when it was hard. The only thing I have ever known for certain is that I was meant to walk this earth with the two of you.

INTRODUCTION

We would like to open this book the same way we start every professional development session we offer: *Thank you.* We love educators, and we are educators. We know how much pressure you are under and just how big your job is. We are grateful for your attention and dedication to your students, families, and each other. And in an ever-changing political and social climate where expectations and demands are continuously shifting, we are particularly grateful for your commitment to improving your antiracist practice.

We are excited to share some ideas and strategies that have moved us closer to being the white antiracist educators we want to be. We are always striving to narrow the gaps between how we want to show up and what we actually do. The great news is that the more we have understood our socialization as white people and stepped into antiracist teaching practices, the more aligned we have felt between who we believe ourselves to be, our intentions, and the impact we are having in school communities.

Power is invested in replicating and protecting itself. The more the racial disparities in this country become impossible to reason away, the greater the fear and unwillingness to uncover that truth. Whether it be the campaign against critical race theory or attacks against "antipatriotic curriculum," the resistance to antiracism is not new; it just changes and morphs to meet the current political climate. But now perhaps more than ever, we need to be clear on what we are teaching and why so we can meet the persistent challenges and, ultimately, end them in the name of doing what is best for our children. *All* of our children.

We want this text to give readers tools for expanding their own practices via inquiry, activities, and examples from our experiences with schools across the country. We offer some points of reflection and some case studies in hopes of demystifying the often-daunting idea of being a less-racist educator and illuminating what the next right step might be. We wrote this with white teachers and white parents in mind. If you are a Person of Color, we hope you find some strategies for working with your white colleagues along with validation of your experiences within a pernicious and maddening white-dominant culture.

For too long, white educators have relied on People of Color to make changes to a relentlessly racist system. This transformational work is ours. But to be clear, we cannot do this in an echo chamber. Over 80% of teachers in this country are white, and given our dominance and its accompanying short-sightedness, we will never be able to fully determine our effectiveness. We must follow the leadership of and be accountable to People of Color in antiracism work. And white people need to commit to shifting our behavior so that our change is observable to People of Color. You will see that we rely on the voices and scholarship of both People of Color and white people because meaningful change can happen only in multiracial coalitions when we are able to stand in true solidarity with each other.

Understanding how we have been shaped by race starts to unravel the harm that is caused by being either oblivious or complacent. It also helps to bring into relief what is at stake for us personally. We cannot simply want to fight racism to help others; it is not "community service" that we do when we have the time or when it feels comfortable. It must be a stance, a perspective that includes our own desire for freedom from the cost of racism for it to be sustainable. We do this with the hope that as educators, we can recognize, affirm, and learn from the humanity and brilliance of all of our students, educators, and families. We write this so that white adults can become mirrors of white antiracism to model a different way forward for white students. We want to encourage and support greater racial literacy for white people so that, perhaps one day, this conversation will no longer be necessary.

In our interviews and work with young people around the country, we have seen firsthand an inability among white students to talk about race without exhibiting significant stress. Of course, there are white children who express curiosity and excitement about learning more about race. They have so many great questions! Yet, we also hear white children as young as nine years old express anxiety about being white and what they think that means. Often, white students, who have volunteered to be interviewed, feel ill equipped and sometimes unable to engage in racial conversations. Many say they "don't think it's their place" to comment on racial issues. It seems that we are successfully raising the next generation of white people to continue to feel afraid and reluctant to talk about race.

For centuries in this country, People of Color have been telling white people about their experiences of race and racism. Yet, white people continue to deny, deflect, and question the validity of their testimony. This resistance is in part due to the overwhelming nature of racism and white people's inability to see how they can be part of the solution. Of course, there are the overt white supremacists who continue to rely on false notions of racial superiority to support their racism. But the vast majority of educators we work with don't wake up in the morning and say, "Who can I be racist toward today?" They tend to go in one of two directions when confronted with evidence of racial bias: Either they assert that racism is all over now and want to recognize all the progress we have made. Or they are reduced to a puddle of guilt and shame. And if they have done some of their own work on challenging racism, they may point to their "racist colleagues" without any sense of how they, too, may be supporting racial inequity on their campus.

What do all these responses have in common? A failure to locate ourselves as agents of change. Embedded in these deflections is an underlying sense that race is something People of Color have, and racism is something they have to endure. If I am not a white supremacist walking around with a Confederate flag draped over my shoulder— one of those "bad" white people—then I'm not the problem. I can feel bad about racism and know that it may be an issue, but I have no understanding of my role because I'm not in the picture. I haven't located myself, my white identity, as part of the equation. I'm still on the sidelines, unsure of the position I should play.

For us, our conversations with other white people about their racial identity and how they see themselves as white gave us a way to understand our role in antiracist teaching and learning. We spent many years trying to understand race via People of Color, and while hearing about their experiences was critical to knowing the realities of racism, it took mentorship from other white antiracists for us to start to see our participation in the system. We remember a Colleague of Color who said, "You will never know what it's like to be a Person of Color. But if you can figure out what it means to be white, then you will understand how to fight racism." That's when the light bulb went on.

To develop a sense of our racial reality, white people need to reflect, describe, and make meaning of whiteness with each other and render it visible. We see this work together not as a replacement for cross-racial dialogue, but as a necessary addition to our engagement with People of Color. Most white people are way behind in their racial identity development. We have years of catch-up work to do to develop the knowledge and skills that antiracism requires. We often think about significant working relationships we have had with Educators of Color who have been aware of their racial identity for their whole lives. Yet, we can tell you where we were when we figured out that we were white and that it meant something, and this realization often happens well into adulthood for most white people. So, we need to work together as white people to be ready and equipped to fight racism. This enables us to move from helping People of Color deal with racism to seeing that it's really *our* problem to address and dismantle.

This book is a guide to lead white educators, leaders, students, and parents toward greater clarity and the development of an explicit, skills-based antiracist practice. We will share relevant research, our experiences working with school/district communities, and strategies and tools that can empower white educators to be part of creating a more equitable educational system for all students. We believe that racial equity will not be fully realized until white educators recognize first their role in supporting a racist system and then their crucial role in dismantling it. Our work with educators across the country has convinced us that we can create antiracist classrooms, but only if we are willing to examine long-held beliefs and to challenge the status quo.

The Shoulders We Stand On

It was the first edition of Dr. Beverly D. Tatum's seminal work *Why Are All the Black Kids Sitting Together in the Cafeteria? And Other Conversations About Race* that grounded our work in racial identity development. Tatum's scholarship was so impactful when first published in 1997 because she took the identity development work from the field of psychology and applied it to schools and students. Her 2017 edition includes an updated introduction that looks at what has transpired since the book was first published, and she did substantive updates to most of the chapters. This is still one of the core texts we recommend and think every white teacher should read. In particular, we owe a great debt to the research Dr. Janet Helms did on white racial identity development, which Tatum describes (1992), and you will see specific references to Helms's work in Chapters 1 and 2 to illustrate how white people come to understand how they are raced.

In *White Women, Race Matters: The Social Construction of Whiteness*, Ruth Frankenberg (1993) delineated a three-part definition of whiteness that has been instrumental to our understanding of how whiteness operates:

1. A *location* of structural advantage, of race privilege
2. A *standpoint*, a place from which white people look at ourselves, at others, and at society
3. A set of *cultural practices* that are usually unmarked and unnamed

Frankenberg (1993) refers to these as "linked dimensions" of whiteness, and they have helped us to better see and name how whiteness shows up and affects our attitude, language, and behavior. We are not using the term "Caucasian" because it was coined to justify biological or scientific racism. It referred to people who came from the Caucasus Mountains region who had a particular physiognomy deemed the most beautiful and desirable. It was one of several so-called racial classifications and is not an accurate description of what we address here. People often prefer to use this term as a way of avoiding the word "white."

Howard Stevenson's work on racial literacy—the ability to identify and resolve racially stressful social interactions—has been foundational in our support of both adults and students. White people can be so overwhelmed by feelings of fear and incompetence that they will avoid conflict and allow racial bias to go unchecked, usually at the expense of Students of Color. His process for naming racial stress and its impacts help to resolve interpersonal interactions and to create healthier school climates.

Shelly Tochluk's book *Witnessing Whiteness* has been a mentor text, especially in times when we had few white antiracist role models. Tochluk (2010) offers concrete examples and individual narratives that have served as touch points in our personal racial development.

To be an effective "threat to inequity," Paul Gorksi focuses on the skills and knowledge that white educators need to challenge racism. His work has helped us move educators from the notion that some people are "just good at talking about race" to the realization that everyone can improve their ability to challenge racism. Gorski's work on equity literacy and his case study approach provide critical frames for the processes we describe here.

Common Language and Concepts

The title we chose, *Learning and Teaching While White,* reflects where we have been and where we want to go. So often, white people feel compelled to question the existence of racism and the testimony of People of Color and to look for other possible explanations for what has taken place, often asking, "Is this really about race?" We know because we did it. For years. We still do it from time to time. The inequities that exist in our school communities mirror the larger racial disparities that have always been a part of US culture. Of course, it *is* about race. But we see how hard white educators struggle to really understand how they might be supporting racism.

We hope this text will help white people shift away from questioning the lived experiences of Students, Teachers, and Families of

Color and toward acknowledging how race, especially ours, and racism impact our educational contexts. There is so much for white people to learn in all directions. While teachers don't often feel like they have significant institutional power to challenge racist systems, we all have a sphere of influence where we can locate our antiracist work. To exercise the power to dismantle racism, we need to develop skills, gain knowledge, and build a practice of reflection. We will show many of the ways that we have been socialized *not* to think about our racial identity as a collective way to address racism. Yet, we have come to realize that the only way to truly interrupt the status quo is to be clear about how our whiteness impacts teaching and learning and to band together as agents of change.

Race is a social construct that divides people into distinct groups by categorizing them based on arbitrary elements of physical appearance, particularly skin color. Most often, race is used when talking about Native, Black/African American, Latinx, Asian American/Pacific Islander, and Middle Eastern people. People of Color is useful as a term because it acknowledges the overall shared experiences of racism. However, the term is also complicated in that it conflates the wide range of very diverse ethnic and racial groups of people into one group and thus obscures their specific histories, experiences, and challenges. As with all racial terms, the interplay between self-identity and identification within the larger social–political context is critical.

It's important to take a close look at white racial identity in the hopes of uncovering and naming what usually passes for "normal." Just as with other racial groups, whiteness is not a singular experience; it is a process of cultural development that is socially constructed and that encompasses many ways of being white. By "socially constructed," we mean that race is not an essential characteristic but rather a social category. We understand whiteness in relation to other people, and whiteness is produced or constructed by our interactions with friends, the media, literature, religious institutions, family, and teachers. *White supremacy* is the belief in the assumed superiority of white people in mainstream society. As a political ideology, it aims to maintain institutional, social, cultural, historical, and political white dominance.

Instead of the term "colorblindness," we will refer to *color-evasiveness,* the ways that white people avoid talking about race by saying, "I don't see color." Of course, unless you are actually colorblind, we all see color and skin tone. Noticing race is not the problem. But a white person thinks that if they can pretend they don't see race, then they can't be accused of being racist.

We also refer to racial *stereotypes*, generalized beliefs or attitudes applied to an entire group of people based on some aspect of their socially-defined group identity—often with little to no experience with the stereotyped group. Stereotypes can lead to *prejudice*, a negative opinion, use of language, or behavior directed at a particular racial group or any person perceived to be a member of that group. *Racism* is a form of discrimination based on racial stereotyping and prejudice (conscious or unconscious, active or passive) that is backed by significant institutional power. We often share the following equation to challenge notions of "reverse racism": racial prejudice + privilege + power = racism (see Appendix C for a visual diagram of these concepts). So, while a Person of Color could be prejudiced toward a white person, there is not a location of structural power held by People of Color that could systematically deny white people opportunities or resources based on their race. Racism is operating when intentional or unintentional barriers impact People of Color's ability to access rights, resources, representation, and respect. Racism indicates the presence of oppressive beliefs and attitudes that the dominant, white group embeds into policies, practices, laws, and systems, consciously or subconsciously.

Tatum (2017) provides a useful metaphor for *antiracism*. She describes racism as a moving walkway. Some people jump on and walk briskly to the end of the walkway. Those would be the "active" racists, your KKK members and Proud Boys. Most just step on the walkway and are carried to the end, the "passive" racists who don't see themselves as racist because they don't use racial slurs nor hate People of Color. The problem is, whether active or passive, we are all carried along by the walkway to the same place. So, to really challenge racism, to be antiracist, we have to turn around and walk at a faster pace, or even run, in the other direction to end up somewhere different and to disrupt the status quo—and maybe to even dismantle the walkway altogether.

While our focus here is on race, we recognize that our racial identity intersects with other aspects of our experiences. *Intersectionality*, as described by Dr. Kimberlé Crenshaw (1991), analyzes how race, class, gender, and other individual characteristics "intersect" with one another and overlap. Her work looked at the intersection of race and gender for Black women in a number of legal cases. To see just their race or just their gender would obscure the impact of *both* racism and sexism on their experiences. Power operates within all social categories with differential effects, and there is complexity to social identity that shapes how we approach antiracist education. We recognize that experiences of whiteness can certainly be impacted by other identifiers, such as gender and social class. As two white women, we think a lot about how our gender impacts our racial identity. Yet, we also know that one of the ways white people avoid looking at race is to focus on other aspects of their identity that are not dominant in society. So, our priority here will be race and, in particular, the experience of whiteness.

We will frequently toggle between talking about the *individual* and the *system*; the two are inextricably linked. Individuals create, reinforce, replicate, and support racist beliefs, relationships, and culture. Any attempt to change the system without also understanding how the system has shaped and informed the individual is doomed to replicate it. We must know the system and our place in it to stand in solidarity with People of Color and to imagine and create something better. While we may refer to something as institutional or systemic racism, it is also a call for white people to consider how we are part of the structure and to take responsibility for dismantling it. And when we use the term "white people," we are always including ourselves.

Overview of Chapters

This book is divided into two parts. "Part I: Preparing for Action—Reflection, Reframing, and New Understandings" includes our introduction and the first three chapters. Here we establish important frameworks and our premise for the text. Chapter 1 explores many of the reasons that whiteness goes unnamed and unmarked in the United States and how white culture has become synonymous with normalcy and even "American-ness." This distorted view of our racial identity has created significant blind spots, what we call "foggy mirrors." We explore why we need to name whiteness as well as its effects on individuals and educational systems so that we have the clarity to take meaningful and intentional action against racism and move toward antiracism. Chapter 2 uses Janet Helms's white racial identity scale to locate and describe the ways white educators move through their racial identity development with examples from our experiences to help illustrate each stage. Chapter 3 applies Helms's statuses to institutional practices and analyzes how whiteness and racism operate in school systems. Just as individuals are raced, educational institutions move through their own racialized stages via their cultures, climates, and procedures. By identifying where a school is in its efforts to challenge racism, we can more effectively target specific steps for intervention and implement enduring antiracist policies and practices.

The second part of the book, "Part II: Steps for Action—Antiracist Strategies for Educational Communities," offers examples for educators, leaders, and parents to forge a new definition of whiteness so we can support all students, especially white students who are in need of models of what white antiracism looks, sounds, and feels like. Chapter 4 looks at how we can build our own consciousness and ability to act without burdening People of Color. We will share examples of best practices, including the role of white antiracist affinity groups. We have found that the creation of these spaces allows for a different kind of identity development—one that is less polarizing and more constructive. Rather than trying to decide if we are "racist" or "not racist," basically "bad" white people or "good" white people, we are able to create a space where educators and students can explore their own identity, understand how bias affects expectations, and learn how to interrupt racism. Chapter 5 reviews pedagogical approaches and curricular topics. We share a variety of lesson plans and strategies for teaching about racial identity, difference, unfairness, and actions to support racial justice. Chapter 6 looks specifically at assessment, including a study we did of how racial identity impacts both the quality and tone of feedback to students. In Chapter 7, we discuss effective leadership practices for developing accountability measures and principled relationships with People of Color. We have also included a chapter for white parents, as we often do parent education in schools, and we have a strong parent following on our *Teaching While White* blog and podcast series. Chapter 8 describes how we support families in having conversations about white racial identity at home and how white parents can support racial justice work in schools.

Our Framework

One unique feature of our approach is the framework we have developed for our professional development work; we refer to it as our "WhAT Questions" (*wh*ite *a*ntiracist *t*eaching), and they are detailed below. We have found that an inquiry stance, paired with our particular scope and sequence, allows educators to move toward an antiracist practice that is both sustainable and replicable, meaning teachers can serve as role models for others.

WhAT Questions: What should I be asking myself, my colleagues, my students, and my school?
1. How does racial diversity in a classroom support learning outcomes? (Value of racial difference)
2. How do we come to understand what it means to be white? (Racial identity development)
3. What gets in the way of healthy racial identity development? (System of racism/internalized dominance)
4. Where and how do racist attitudes, language, and behavior show up in schools? (Identification and data)
5. How do we address racial stereotypes and racism? (Skill development)
6. How can we create and model antiracist pedagogy and curricula? (Teaching/coaching practices)

Each question establishes a site for reflection, inquiry, dialogue, and action. For example, with the first question, we find that many institutions are still making a *moral* argument for their racial equity work and have not yet connected the dots between excellent teaching, engaged student learning, and racial equity. While the work of racial justice is certainly related to morality, that has not been enough to shift the status quo. There are still two distinct efforts happening on most campuses: the daily work of the school and core functions (such as curriculum development and assessment) on one hand and efforts at what is often referred to as "diversity, equity, and inclusion" (DEI) on the other (an assembly here, a faculty training there, but nothing that is consistent or sustained). We have found that institutions need to explore the research and practices that have shown that racially diverse learning environments support greater critical thinking, creativity, and problem-solving skills. Teachers need to know how their unexamined racial biases can affect the expectations they have of their students, which will in turn affect achievement in their classes. We will return to this framework in Chapter 6 so you can see how we use it from a leadership perspective.

Voices in the Text

For most of the book, we will use the pronoun "we" to signify our personal but collective experiences as white people and as white educators. There will be times when we will note that our two perspectives or experiences diverge. The following bios provide more context for our positionality and how we have come to understand our whiteness and its relationship to each of our teaching and learning.

From Elizabeth:

This book has been a long time in the making for me. Patterns emerged early in my teaching that left me wondering about my role in the educational system and how racism might be operating in my own classroom. But those patterns were illusory and initially hard to describe. They appeared in what seemed to be random examples, yet taken together, a picture began to emerge.

When I was teaching in California in the late 1990s, some of my high school students hosted affinity group discussions on ethnic and racial identity. Signs were posted in the lunchroom telling students where their affinity group would meet. A white student leader and I waited patiently in the classroom designated for Euro-American/white students and teachers. No one else came to this meeting. After lunch, as I was debriefing with the student leaders, one of my Students of Color turned to me and said, with a look of disbelief: "Do white people know they are white?" It was an excellent question, and we spent the next half hour trying to think of ways we could help white people see their race as an essential part of diversity and antiracism.

In my English class elective, called Ethnic Voices, we explored the social construction of racial and ethnic identity by analyzing texts and in engaging in self-reflection. I always started the class by asking students to identify and write about the first time they became aware of their race. The white students stared at me blankly. One raised her hand and said, "But I don't have a race. I'm just regular." If asked the same question when I was their age, my reply would have been the same. I was raised to be "colorblind" and to not "see" race. Well into my twenties, I believed that to notice race was to be racist.

For me, both of these scenarios describe a key feature of racism in schools. Without a clear understanding of who we are as individuals, how can we possibly come to know and value others? And if we cannot name who and what we are, we might define ourselves by what we are *not*: white students seeing themselves as *not raced*. This leaves a huge gap between those who have a racial identity and those who do not, a space that creates divisions between people that are arbitrary and artificial. It is also a convenient way of abdicating responsibility for racial tension, prejudice, and violence. If a white student—or teacher—locates herself as normal and average, then diversity is not for her. Another example emerged when a new high school group called Student Nation was organized to affirm student identity and to help build a coalition of several existing ethnic groups. Many white students said to me, "I can't join. I'm not a Person of Color." "Diversity" had become a synonym for racialized minorities, and as long as white students and teachers could deny their race, the gap between them and People of Color would continue to widen. It was then that I decided to really focus on opening up conversations of understanding race and racism with my white students and colleagues.

From Jenna:

Though I was aware of being white from an early age, I had little to no understanding how my race had any broader or significant meaning. It wasn't until much later that I had any concept of power, privilege, or oppression in relationship to my identity. My awareness of these larger systems came through my work within nonprofits; and even then, it was through the lenses of sexism and classism—a racial lens would come later.

Once I became a teacher, I was often charged with doing DEI (diversity, equity, and inclusion) work at the school because of my experience working with marginalized groups in nonprofits, though really my racial consciousness was just starting to develop. Looking back, I believe this was when I did the most racial harm because I was trusted and believed to be progressive—one of the "good" ones. I had little cause to doubt what I thought I knew. However, it was my work with students that changed that.

It wasn't really through a specific interaction but through several interactions I had with my students over time that I became interested in how identity impacts teaching and learning. How does my identity influence what I choose to teach? How does the identity of my students impact how they experience the curriculum? How do they perceive our interactions based on who they are, and how does my identity impact my perceptions of those same encounters? I started having conversations about these questions with other teachers. We decided to collaborate and create a national learning conference where we could better understand our context and where teachers could find meaningful answers to their questions about race. As a collective, we started the Multicultural Teaching Institute (MTI) to look at issues of identity development in the classroom with a primary focus on race.

What I saw again and again—at MTI, at school, and in conversations about race in general—was that the focus was always on Black and Brown students, colleagues, and families. I understood that over 80% of educators were white, yet I rarely heard anyone name or analyze how whiteness was a factor when talking about racial dynamics in education. I started to seek out stories to see if there were "best practices" in making whiteness explicit, and this put me on the trajectory toward my project with Elizabeth, *Teaching While White*, a blog and podcast series focused on making whiteness visible and challenging racism in school communities. In this pursuit, I have become equally interested in the relationship between racial self-awareness and the ability to take effective action toward change.

At times it is comical how differently we approach racial conflict. Elizabeth is more extroverted and has an analytical mind, whereas I am more introverted and tend to think more laterally. When we are asked in workshops how we would respond to a tense racial moment, we often gasp to hear how the other would approach the situation. There are multiple styles and pathways, and we have developed our particular strategies over time and across varied contexts. We will keep our distinct voices where necessary because we ultimately believe in the strength that comes from diversity, even our own.

The Value of Humility

We have come to value each of our approaches and now see the benefits of many ways of understanding racial identity and challenging racism. There is no right way to undo what is a huge, adaptive system of oppression, no single blueprint or proven ten-step plan. Yet, there is so much anger, frustration, and self-righteousness between white people within antiracist groups, efforts, and movements. While we should be open to feedback and we need to be accountable for the antiracist work we do, there is a great deal of competition between white educators for who can prove themselves to be the most "woke." Over many decades, we have watched white people try to one-up each other and be the smartest person in the room when it comes to talking about race. When we are busy critiquing, questioning, and discrediting the work of other white people, we are not fighting the real enemy: racism. When we are busy trying to show someone else how racist they are by calling out their mistake for all to see, we risk alienating other white people and leaving it for our Colleagues of Color to deal with their racism. We need to engage, not accuse. Professor Loretta Ross suggests that we call each other "in" to challenging conversations about race and racism. Calling in is like calling out, but it is done privately and with respect. "It's a call out done with love," she said. That may mean simply sending someone a private message or even ringing them on the telephone (!) to discuss the matter or simply taking a breath before commenting, screen-shotting, or demanding one "do better" without explaining how.

———

Instead of assuming the worst, we can demonstrate compassion. *And that doesn't mean we ignore or downplay any racial harm.* It just means we are committed to *engaging* other white people and helping each other to cause less pain. Instead of scrutinizing others and deciding what work *they* need to do, we need to be intentional about our own need for growth. Instead of leaning away from a colleague who just made a racist statement, we commit to reaching out and having a conversation about why what they said was racially problematic. It requires deep humility, something we have come to value as an essential anti-racist skill. Yet many white people display great arrogance when confronted with their own racism. We hope this text serves as a calling in to white educators to challenge racism in their educational institutions. It has been our privilege to do this work alongside each other, our white colleagues, and our Colleagues of Color, all of whom remain committed to a vision of multiracial solidarity and the possibility of racial justice in education.

LEARNING AND TEACHING WHILE WHITE

PART I

PREPARING FOR ACTION

—

REFLECTION, REFRAMING, AND NEW UNDERSTANDINGS

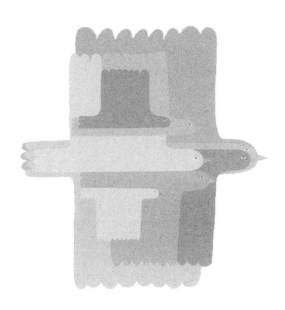

CHAPTER I

Foggy Mirrors

Everyone suffers when white people are unaware and uninformed about race and racism. People of Color have always known the destruction that comes not just from the intentional racist but from white people who believe themselves to be good, liberal allies. Though we believe that no educator goes into the field with a purpose of hurting people, we know that harm comes from white teachers who, like us, wanted to "help" the next generation. For far too long, we have remained unaware of ourselves as racial beings and unconscious of our internalized superiority and have therefore upheld racist systems and thinking. In this way, our inability to see race in ourselves impairs our ability to see others clearly. It becomes like a funhouse of mirrors wherein we catch distorted or fractured images of ourselves without seeing the full picture.

The inability of white individuals to see and name the truth of how racism lives in us and the way we take desperate measures to avoid seeing it, let alone claiming it, echoes throughout our institutions and our country's history. White people as a group have not told the truth of the violence and oppression that white dominance requires now or has required in the past. We have collectively lacked the will to dispel American myths about race and racial history—including the lies embedded in the culture at our nation's founding. Our Declaration of Independence, to take the most glaring example, invokes the "unalienable rights" of "life, liberty and the pursuit of happiness" as reasons for the colonies' independence while these very same colonists stood on stolen land and offered no such dignity to the human beings who had been living here for 10,000 or more years. The Declaration of Independence also pronounces that "all men are created equal" while most of our founding fathers enslaved Black people. Yet to date, educational institutions still downplay this racist dichotomy in our history and institutions or excuse such behavior because it was the common practice at the time.

Of course, the erasure of historical truth also threatens the grasp on reality for white people. Once the myths were solidly planted and reinforced, many white people came to believe that the country's, and their own accomplishments and progress, are *owed* to them. When presented with more accurate information about race, white people may start to believe that they are under threat and that *their* history and identity are at risk of being erased. Across the country, many white parents are raising concerns that teaching their children about race and naming whiteness in schools is equivalent to shaming their kids and making them feel guilty. Allowing white people to believe that they are at the center of everything and reinforcing those misperceptions is, to a different degree, another way of upholding racism.

During workshops on racial identity and the role of white educators in challenging racism with each other, we have heard questions from countless white educators like, "Are we *ever* going to get to how we help our Students of Color?" and "How do we move away from our navel gazing so we can dismantle the system?" and "Can we just focus on changing our curriculum?" We have both posed similar questions, whether fueled by frustration or the need to identify ourselves as "getting it." We fully recognize the urgency and desire to fix things, but without a developed racial consciousness of ourselves, we both have created bigger messes in our wake as we attempted to make structural change.

To be clear, self-reflection does not replace nor come at the cost of taking action, but that self-awareness is the key to envisioning systems outside of the racist structures we have been socialized by. White people can only stand in solidarity with, take leadership from, and develop authentic relationships with those who are most impacted by racism—People of Color—if they know how *they* have been racialized. We often hear from schools who are eager to look at systems, policies, and curriculum and to start evaluating them for racial equity. Yes, we absolutely want schools to make these changes, AND when white people in positions of power continue to view themselves as exempt and to not understand how they are often upholding and reproducing racism, efforts to make systemic change become a game of whack-a-mole. Racism will just show up somewhere else. We also want to challenge the notion that teachers can't be biased, something we hear frequently. It's probably the number one defense we observe when we work with schools. It goes something like this:

> "I love all my kids. I don't care if they're blue, green, brown, or purple."

> "I have committed my life to serving these kids."

> "We are a very diverse school."

> "We have done a lot of work to make our curriculum more reflective of Students of Color. We added in a bunch of new books for our read-alouds."

Eduardo Bonilla-Silva's (2009) research and analysis in *Racism Without Racists* documents this pattern of "colorblind racism" where white people really struggle to see their participation in a racist system when they see themselves as "nice" and "good." From their vantage point, racism is about overt, evil acts by white supremacists. The ways that they may be supporting those systems remain invisible. Yet, to deny difference is to deny the impact that race has on people's lives. In contrast to saying there are no differences at all among people, color evasion is a selective attention to difference, saying that color does not matter. In this way, a white woman who is not comfortable talking about race can selectively avoid the topic and instead focus on differences that she is comfortable with. This is simply another kind of oppression disguised as polite discourse. It is this selective engagement with difference that exposes color evasion as a way of maintaining the power and privilege of the dominant group. The white woman in this example has the privilege of not seeing her color or its impact, and, subsequently, denying others their racial identity.

Color evasion can play a role in a subtle but insidious kind of racism termed "aversive racism," and as Beverly Tatum (1997) notes, aversive racists have "internalized the espoused cultural values of fairness and justice for all at the same time that they have been breathing the 'smog' of racial biases and stereotypes pervading the popular culture" (p. 118). Color aversion masks itself as nonbiased, but since one group is free to ignore the racial identity of another, discrimination exists. Thus, a seemingly nonprejudiced stance has major power implications. Here, the denial of race locates a desire to be fair next to the power to discriminate. If it is clear what the right thing to do is, aversive racists will act in a way that supports their nonprejudiced view of themselves. However, if a situation is not clear and an action can be justified based on some factor other than race, prejudiced feelings toward People of Color will surface.

Tatum (1997) gives an excellent example of how this subtle form of bias manifests. White college students were given transcripts and asked to evaluate candidates for admission to their college. The qualifications of all the transcripts presented to the white students were equal; the only difference was the race of the candidate. The study found that when the transcript indicated that students were not qualified, Black and white students were both rejected, irrespective of race. When the candidates were somewhat qualified, white students were favored over Black students by a slim margin. However, when the candidates were *highly* qualified, the white students overwhelmingly chose white candidates. So, even when all qualifications are equal, applicants were not perceived as equal, especially when both Black and white applicants were highly qualified. Blacks were good, but whites were better.

The "Teachers Are People Too" study from Princeton and Tufts (Starck et al., 2020) shows that teachers are just as likely to have racial bias as nonteachers. Using data gathered by the Implicit Association Tests, researchers showed that 77% of teachers have biases that they are unwilling or unable to name (implicit bias) as compared to 77.1% of nonteachers. And teachers show just about the same level of explicit bias as nonteachers (about 30%). The results of the study suggested that although teachers may be more well-intentioned than the general population, they still have bias that needs to be addressed because it impacts the expectations they have of students, the quality of their teaching, and the ways they manage behavior and discipline.

The inability to see ourselves beyond our intentions also impacts our ability to work with and take leadership from People of Color. Nora Erakat and Paul Gorski (2019) did a series of studies that examined the causes of burnout in racial justice activists. They found that many Activists of Color cited the behaviors and attitudes of white racial justice activists as a major source of their burnout: "they shared how they grew emotionally and physically exhausted coping with the ways white activists carried their privilege and entitlement into racial justice movements—how it deteriorated their well-being, contributing to their burnout" (p. 786). The study uncovered how white racial activists often continued to hold unevolved racist views; undermined, invalidated, or took credit for the efforts of People of Color; and showed an ongoing unwillingness to step up and take action. Yes, white people need to take action *and* we need to continue to develop our racial consciousness and never assume that we are "woke" or that we have arrived at some pinnacle of racial competence.

Many People of Color understand this well. In *No Name in the Street* (1972), James Baldwin describes the danger that comes of white people being afraid to do the interior work of racial self-awareness:

> *If Americans were not so terrified of their private selves, they would never have needed to invent and could never have become so dependent on what they still call "the Negro problem." This problem, which they invented in order to safeguard their purity, has made of them criminals and monsters, and it is destroying them; and this not from anything blacks may or may not be doing but because of the role a guilty and constricted white imagination has assigned to the blacks. . . . People pay for what they do, and, still more, for what they have allowed themselves to become. And they pay for it very simply:*

by the lives they lead. The crucial thing, here, is that the sum of these individual abdications menaces life all over the world. (p. 34)

At a recent speaking engagement, we took a question from a white woman who asked, "How do you respond to anger from your children when they learn of injustices and systemic racism?" Not fully understanding the question, we asked her to clarify, and it became clear that she wanted to shield her child from anger, seeing it as dangerous and unproductive. There is, of course, privilege in that question. Which children get to be shielded from truths that might make them angry (or worse) and question their value, beauty, intelligence, and own knowledge? It is appropriate to be angry. For all of us to be angry. White people have been duped, lulled, and encouraged to remain "neutral" when teaching about difficult subjects like racism, and we have been uninvolved and ignorant of racial harm. We need white people's outrage to fuel and propel change. Anger can be used as motivation to know and do more, as long as we do not get stuck there, and it affords us an opportunity to step into our integrity, to change the story and how it unfolds.

Students Do as We Do, Not as We Say

There is a common cultural myth that racism is diminishing among youth today, but we continually meet with white students who are unaware that incidents of racism are currently on the rise. When we do not give language to and discuss race in educational settings, we leave students, particularly white students who are often not discussing race at home, vulnerable as they try to make sense of the heavily racialized world they see and experience daily. In the absence of accurate information about race, students rely on what is available to them: media and stereotypes, which typically support extremely harmful myths about the superiority or inferiority of intellect, ability, and even humanity of different races.

Daily, Students of Color, more often than not, must grapple with and understand their racial identity and encounter race-based stress within a white-dominated world. Yet many white students often make it through their school careers never knowing that they, too, have a race, and that whiteness impacts the way they move through the world. If white students are never made aware of their own racial identity and they never understand that it impacts their standing in the world, then their racial identity is never explicit. It remains obscured in that feeling that only Students of Color have a race—that they are *different*—and once again whiteness passes for normal. Therefore, mirrors that should be clear remain foggy, and that haze creates all kinds of misunderstandings and missteps that cause harm.

The role of educators in conversations about race becomes even more important given that the first time many children will talk about their racial identity may be at school. Yet, if the only time race is mentioned in school is when we are talking about oppression—enslavement, internment camps, the civil rights movement, etc.—Children of Color only see their identity represented in a negative context, and white children are left with only racist portrayals of white people. This leaves white students vulnerable to the messages of white supremacists groups that are actively recruiting white students, and white boys in particular, offering the comfort of slogans such as, "It's OK to be white!"

All students need to be able to discuss racial issues with a healthy understanding of the history and complexity of systemic racism—to know that it is not about "good" or "bad" white people and not about individual acts of meanness. As Ali Michael says in her TedTalk, "How Can I Have a Positive Racial Identity? I'm White," a healthy white racial identity is not about feeling bad about being white. It is also not about feeling good about being white. It is about understanding that whiteness is not peripheral to who we are. We need our students to understand that race is integral to who we are as white people and not just something People of Color have.

In the absence of explicit and direct instruction about race and racism, our white students tend to develop a confused and negative view about racial matters. It is also true that if we don't start early with white students, they will not develop age-appropriate understandings of racial identity and difference. In fact, when white students are asked to engage in conversations about race and racism—which commonly doesn't happen until the later elementary years or even in middle school—they frequently display defensiveness in the form of anxiety and vulnerability. They describe feeling "unsafe" in conversations about race, believing they will say the wrong thing and get "in trouble." Many white students feel attacked, as though they are being made to feel guilty any time race enters the conversation. And because the best defense is a good offense, we hear white students complain about another "diversity day" and lament that conversations about race are being "forced down their throats." They are nervous and uncomfortable, and they have no idea what to do with those feelings.

Teaching white children about whiteness can be challenging because there has always been a strong social norm in US society that sanctions white people who talk explicitly about race. And the notion of calling ourselves "white," as opposed to some ethnic designation like Italian or Irish, is the same as being a member of the Ku Klux Klan. It just isn't done because typically the only association we have with "white" is "racist." This norm, shared widely among white people, has a profound effect. It not only keeps racism firmly in place, it also keeps white people from understanding that they have a race and, thus, some responsibility or agency around ending racism.

Without any mirrors to reflect their race and experiences, Students of Color spend a lot of energy navigating whiteness, the dominant culture. Meanwhile, the white students are just swimming along in the water they know so well—or rather that they don't even see because it is just that; the air they breathe. So, while the white students' experience is reflected all around them, the reflection is nebulous. It's foggy because it is never named for what it is: white identity, unearned privilege, and power.

Clearer Reflections

The ability to eradicate racism and revolutionize our educational communities is predicated on the ability to see and identify an *accurate* reflection of who we are as white people at the individual, interpersonal, institutional, and cultural levels, beginning with ourselves. To create systemic change, we need enough white people to shift for our society to truly transform. This is both good news and bad news. If you are reading this book, it likely indicates that you want change and that you are willing to put in some work (at least some reading) to do it. The difficulty lies in all the ways a true reflection of ourselves and our group membership is obscured by the privilege of not having to see and notice racial inequity. The system has been built to reinforce its dominance and to generate the fog that affects our ability to see our role in supporting racism.

If I can't really see myself in the mirror, see *all* the elements of my identity including my race, then I'm left with a partial image. My view is limited and obscured. And race remains something that only People of Color have, and racism is that thing that bad white people do—rinse and repeat. John Biewen, radio documentarian and host of the podcast series *Seeing White*, spoke in an interview about his need to strengthen his "letting go muscle" (Tippett, 2020). He described the necessity of releasing the stories we tell ourselves about who we are, what we know, and what this country is as a necessary step in developing a racial consciousness. But letting go of the solid ground that we believe our lives and identities are built on is scary. Yet, the investment white people have in holding on to these narratives is largely responsible for holding us back, as individuals and as a country, from the truth that racial healing requires. We must be willing to step out into the unknown if we are to envision something that is truer and more aligned with our integrity.

REFLECTION QUESTIONS

We need to be willing to look at the stories we tell ourselves about who we are in the world. That introspection can help us learn about the nuanced and often complicated truths of long-held personal and family narratives and myths. It can be difficult to let go of some of these stories because letting go may feel like a betrayal of family loyalty, cause division and upset, and/ or produce anger at what we didn't know or realize. Yet, there is a freedom that comes when we do not need to protect or defend distortions and falsehoods anymore. There is a kind of relief that emerges when we see ourselves with greater clarity and authenticity.

1. Is there a part of your narrative about your own racialized life that you need to let go of?
2. How would letting go of that stance change your understanding of yourself? Your family or history?
3. What scares you the most about examining how race has shaped you? What if the worst possible realization came to light? What would happen?
4. If you let it go, what clarity might emerge in its place? What space might you create for new understandings and change?

CHAPTER 2

Talking About Race Means Talking About Whiteness

As experienced teachers, administrators, and now consultants, we spend a lot of time with white teachers and administrators who are completely flummoxed by how to address race and racism in their classrooms and on their campuses. These educators wring their hands, desperate for answers. They plead, "Is there a 10-step plan? Just tell me what to do!" and the perennial, "Don't tell me about a problem without a way to fix it." They are constantly looking for solutions but believe those remedies to be outside of themselves—beyond their sphere of influence. The great irony is that the work to end racist teaching practices *is* the work of white educators. It starts with our own reckoning: we have failed, failed again, made messes, and caused harm and hurt to People of Color around us. We are by no means the first, nor will we be the last, but we want to create a door for other white teachers to walk through.

"The heart of justice is truth telling," writes bell hooks (2018) in her book *All About Love* (p. 33). We believe this, and yet we know everyone has a very different relationship to telling racial truths. I, Jenna, call myself a recovering WASP. I was indoctrinated into a culture that prioritizes manners, making sure everyone is comfortable, and speaking about emotions with nuanced metaphors—definitely *not* truth telling. None of these traits are useful antiracist skills, and in many ways, I have had to work hard to recover pieces of my humanity that

WASPiness hid from me. My WASP upbringing not only encouraged my silence and affability, but also made me mistrustful and avoidant of people who blurted out their emotions and made situations uncomfortable by telling the truth. "Doesn't everyone know a nice little white lie will allow for everyone's comfort and, therefore, safety?" I wondered, quickly followed by, "She must have some kind of emotional issues, parading all her feelings to anyone who will listen!" I was raised with a deep and abiding understanding of public life versus private life, and I remember, with time-defying clarity, what happened when I said or did something publicly that was considered something to be kept private by my family. But I have come to believe that my integrity cannot exist in two separate realms. I have had to unlearn these values and step into doing and saying things that feel like they go against the grain of my socialization no matter where I am.

What many of us have failed to understand is how being racially unconscious hurts white people. There is no possible way to compare the marginalization, trauma, and violence that People of Color experience daily because of racism and the ignorance of white people. But without a clear understanding of the price we pay for colluding with a system that advantages us over People of Color, we avoid any kind of real reckoning. Racism leads white people to believe they are "winning" at something. So, who would dismantle a system that puts them at the top? We may not have an accurate story of our own family histories, making us blind to the ways race impacted our personal development. We unwittingly say and do unkind things to our Friends and Colleagues of Color and then are confused as to why they do not want to be around us. How foolish we are that, despite hundreds of years of testimony, literature, art, and music, white people still question, "Is this really about race?" Another often unconscious behavior emerges when white people hear about a racist incident or their own behavior is called into question. We have witnessed and heard numerous incidents of white people who have become overwhelmed by emotion during conversations about race and use their upset and tears to focus on how hurt they are instead of addressing the injury of racism (Accapadi, 2007). We are unable to take feedback from People of Color and are left to repeat the same mistake over and over again, yet there are ways to break through these destructive patterns.

Moving Toward Greater Consciousness

Establishing a relationship with another white person who can serve as an accountability partner is one way to manage the confusion and overwhelm that can get in the way of productive cross-racial dialogue. This partner is a white colleague who can help us understand how we are participating in the dynamic, not someone who will just tell us how nice we are and how they know we didn't mean to hurt anyone. This partnership helps us to address the impact of our behavior and to not defend our intentions in the moment. Talking through an issue when we feel stressed or overwhelmed gives us an opportunity to process our feelings without further taxing Colleagues of Color. Emotions are important to antiracist work, so we don't just intellectualize and analyze what's going on. However, we need to ensure that our upset brings us *into* the conversation as opposed to derailing it. "Yes, you can see my tears, as this is upsetting, but I don't need to be taken care of right now. Please continue what you were sharing." We must rely on both our reason and our emotion to develop an effective antiracist practice.

Some aspects of our identity may have caused us to be marginalized, and we can use those experiences to better understand the places that we are elevated or have great privilege. In an interview, Robin DiAngelo spoke of her experience of growing up in poverty and how that gave her a pathway in, rather than a way of opting out: "When I use my white position to break with silence and white solidarity and speak up, I am simultaneously healing the lie that I am inherently inferior because I grew up poor. So, for me to center race—even though I experience oppression and have experienced oppression in other aspects of my life—for me to center race and feed every other identity or experience through that lens has been the most profound tool" (Tippett, 2020).

Psychologist Janet Helms (pronounced *Hel-ums*) identified a pattern and later wrote a book on the racial identity development for white people. *A Race Is a Nice Thing to Have: A Guide to Being a White Person or Understanding the White Persons in Your Life* was a transformative text for both of us. Reading her description of the stages that white people go through to confront racism and abandon racist beliefs was perhaps the biggest catalyst for being able to locate ourselves within the construct of race.

In addition to helping us to orient ourselves within having a racial identity, Helms's model has also given us a tool to recognize when we are having a particular racial response or getting stuck believing in a particular perspective. Identifying these moments allows us to step outside of the emotion and confusion that inevitably arise when grappling with race and offers markers of a path forward. It also helped to know that these stages were a pattern predictable enough to document, which meant we were not alone in this nor just some bad outlier. This, in turn, helped us to release the guilt and shame that, though often an inevitable part of racial development, can immobilize us and keep us from challenging racism.

This model has also helped us to identify where *other* white people are in their development and allows us to meet people where they are. When we think of racial awareness as a form of literacy, we do not ask someone who is insisting that they don't see color to examine their white fragility. To do so would be akin to asking someone who is just beginning to read to decode a medical journal.

Perhaps most importantly, being able to identify and recognize these stages in ourselves allows us to feel compassion and patience, instead of judgment and frustration (most of the time) with other white people when we recognize that we ourselves have been in that same place at one time or another. Many white people, when they first start to identify themselves within a white, antiracist identity, call out, question, and shame other white people so that many do not want to take the risk of this kind of punishment. When white people lean away and shun other white people for not understanding the ways they have internalized a racist culture, we, at best, deter white people from engaging further, and at worst, essentially offer incentive for the creation of more white supremacists.

But this dynamic of wanting to be the best antiracist and compete with other white people mostly comes at a cost, once again, to People of Color. When a white person is spurned and feels called out, or even understands that they may have actually hurt someone, it is in direct conflict with how they want to view themselves. As a result, many white people lash out not just to the person who has called them out, but at People of Color in general. White people who feel shamed about their racist behavior or attitudes either double down on why People of Color are the problem or they refuse to engage with topics that could be disruptive to their self-perception—but either way, it amounts to another white person opting out of the conversation.

As teachers, we know that when we have difficulty with a particular student it is often because we see some part of ourselves in that student. The same has been true when working with adults. Becoming more racially conscious has meant a lot of self-reflection and facing uncomfortable things about ourselves. When we recognize the same wounds in other people, it can be difficult for us to act out of love and compassion. We often feel aggravated and impatient. We have learned to ask ourselves some questions when we notice that we are feeling annoyed or angry with another person and feel compelled to let them know. Before calling something into question, we ask ourselves: *Have I done or said the same thing that I am annoyed about? Does offering this feedback give me satisfaction and/or make me feel better than? How would I react if someone said this to me? What is motivating my urge to say this?* This moment of self-reflection can allow for connection and the opportunity to move white people toward greater racial understanding.

Our Identity Development

Below is a brief description of Janet Helms's stages, or statuses, of white racial identity development as summarized by Dr. Beverly Daniel Tatum (2017), with additional points by Dr. Ali Michael, cofounder and director of the Race Institute for K–12 Educators. Helms identifies these first three statuses as abandoning racism and the second three as defining a nonracist white identity. These stages are not linear and can be affected by a particular context: we can be in one stage in one moment and then walk into a situation and move into a totally different stage. We can also be in several stages at once.

Abandonment of Racism

Contact. We are unaware of our own racial identity; we don't think of ourself as "white," but as "normal"; we tend to view racism as "individual acts of meanness" rather than as an institutionalized system and typically do not recognize or acknowledge "white privilege"; and we have a naïve curiosity or fear of People of Color, usually based on stereotypes.

At this stage we:

- generally believe the world is fair, and everyone has equal opportunities;
- are unaware of our whiteness and believe white is a universal way of being that everyone should ascribe to;
- try not to see race: "I'm colorblind"; and
- do not challenge messages of internalized superiority.

Disintegration. Our awareness of racism and white privilege increase as a result of personal experiences; our common emotional responses to this new information include shame, guilt, denial, anger, depression, and withdrawal; and we may attempt to persuade others to abandon racist thinking.

At this stage we:

- have a conscious but conflicted acknowledgment of whiteness; and
- feel caught between racial realities.

Reintegration. We may feel pressure from others to "not notice" racism; our feelings of guilt and denial are transformed into fear and anger toward People of Color and our common response is to "blame the victim"; and we choose to avoid the issue of racism, if possible, rather than struggle to define a nonracist identity.

At this stage:

- our guilt and anxiety are transformed into hostility and anger;
- it feels like there are no right answers: to be white is to be wrong; and
- we have selective attention to stereotype-confirming information.

Percentagewise, many white people live in the reintegration stage because the disintegration stage is the most painful and difficult to navigate.

Defining a Nonracist White Identity

Pseudoindependence. We begin to abandon our beliefs in white superiority; we have an intellectual understanding of the unfairness of white privilege and recognize personal responsibility for dismantling racism; we distance ourself from other whites and actively seek out of People of Color to help us better understand racism.

At this stage we:

- still think about racial issues rather than feeling them;
- depend on People of Color to define racial identity;
- see racism, but may still believe that if People of Color worked harder, racism wouldn't affect them;
- compare oppressions: "My people suffered too"; and
- continue to exhibit a sense of internalized superiority.

Immersion/emersion. We actively seek to redefine whiteness; we ask ourself questions such as "Who am I racially? What does it really mean to be white in the United States?"; we need support from other antiracist whites who have asked similar questions; we focus on developing a positive white identity that is not based on assumed superiority; and we take pride in our active antiracist stance.

At this stage we:

- take more responsibility for racism and privilege;
- move from trying to change People of Color to trying to change racism and ourself;
- may try to immerse ourself in Communities of Color; and
- are critical of ourself and others.

Autonomy. We have internalized a positive white racial identity; we are actively antiracist within own sphere of influence; our racial identity development is not static, and we are open to new information and ongoing self-examination; and we are able to work effectively in multi-racial settings in "beloved community."

At this stage we:

- have a conscious use of privilege and a willingness to take action;
- value true diversity and difference, not just in skin color but in cultural style, dialect, approach to time, etc.;
- seek and accept feedback from Colleagues of Color; and
- understand that racism is systemic and historically rooted.

To provide more context for these various stages, we will share our own experiences navigating Helms's schema. We will describe moments in our racial identity development and link them to one or more particular stages.

Jenna's Story

For me the **contact** stage did not last very long. I lived in a predominantly white neighborhood in Charlottesville, Virginia. Though the city has a large Black population, I lived in an almost entirely white neighborhood, attended a predominantly white church, and went to a preschool that was also predominantly white. I would not have been able to articulate, at such a young age, ideas such as being "colorblind," but I certainly started to hear those messages. Though my parents were activists of a kind, they still believed that to talk about race was racist, so we didn't very often, except in an exoticized way with an almost envious tone, of Black culture in particular. Later, my parents chose to send my sister and I to the local public school, which was one of the very last schools in the country to desegregate.

It was my elementary school experience that propelled me into **disintegration**. I am not certain of the racial makeup of the students, but when I attended Venable in 1974, there were two faculty members of color, including my recently immigrated Japanese music teacher in whose class we learned the cotton-picking song *Jump Down, Turn Around, Pick a Bale of Cotton*. The rest of the teachers were white. I started having Black classmates and friends, and on occasion I would go on playdates to their houses. I had never seen this part of town before, and the neighborhoods were almost entirely Black. The houses were smaller and there was trash in the streets. At school, though I'm certain I could not have articulated it, I understood on some level that the expectations for me and my other white classmates were different than for my Black classmates. I could not make sense of these disparities that clearly fell along racial lines. I went into this highly racially charged environment every day but had no vocabulary, scaffolding, context, or discussion about what I was experiencing.

My well-intentioned, liberal parents and an "integrated" school were not enough to prevent racial stereotypes. In the absence of information, I had to rely on what was available to me—media messages, racial lies, and myths—to make sense of the world I was seeing, and I **reintegrated**. By about the age of 7, I started to believe that Black families and kids must not care about education the way that mine did. That Black neighborhoods existed because they chose it and that they didn't work as hard as white people. I started only playing with the other white students and started (unconsciously) believing in my own racial superiority, though I had been taught to say things like, "Everyone is equal." I even began to fear Black people outside of school.

I cannot pinpoint a specific transition to starting to create a non-racist identity for myself. I dipped into being curious about the racial disparities I knew existed, I cared about my Friends of Color, and I certainly wanted to believe myself to be one of the good white people. I also know that I reintegrated anytime I felt challenged, embarrassed, or ill-informed and avoided talking directly about race with my Friends of Color. I went to a small liberal arts college and wrote my thesis about homelessness and was never once asked to consider how race played a factor in housing security. I went to graduate school to get a master's in cross-cultural education and was only required to take one "diversity" class. I student-taught in the Los Angeles school district and was never prompted, compelled, or questioned to consider either my race nor that of my students.

Later, I did prevention and education work for a domestic violence agency, and it was there that I started to understand sexism as systemic and institutional power. Through this, I started to get a foundational understanding of racism, heterosexism, classism, and all -isms as systems. While my understanding was intellectual and disconnected from my own life, I had enough of an understanding to be dangerous.

I became deeply entrenched in the self-righteousness of **pseudoindependence**. Not only did I distance myself from other white people who I thought "didn't get it," I also tried to hide parts of myself that seemed "too white," like my British father and the British culture that was part of my upbringing. I thought my experiences and my good intentions gave me an authority, and even a responsibility, to point out and shame the lack of understanding that other white people had about racial injustice. I call this my "wokest white woman phase." Later, when I became a teacher, I set about fixing the Kids of Color. I thought it was about helping Students of Color achieve and being a good white person. It wasn't until several years later when I was teaching my then favorite book, *To Kill A Mockingbird,* that I became aware of how delusional this belief was. I had prepared some amazing lessons and believed I was taking on racism head-on. I sat my students down on the floor in a circle so we could have a "real" discussion about racism.

During my meticulously planned lesson, a Black student in my class stood up and walked out of the room. She was shaking, and when I asked her what was wrong, she said that the lesson was making her "a little uncomfortable." Now this really is such a mild interruption of my whiteness, but it did not feel small at the time. I was upset. I dissolved into tears with my colleagues. Instead of hearing and seeing what was going on for my student, I made this about me. Didn't she understand that I was trying to help her by talking about racism? Truthfully, I was probably even a little angry, "She should be grateful for all the ways I was fighting injustice in my classroom."

Eventually, I was able to become curious about my teaching: *How could all my good intentions have gone badly? How did my identity impact how what I taught was received by my students? What didn't I know? What didn't I know that I didn't know?* I became curious about the lives of my students. I stopped relying on the assumptions I had about what their reality was and found ways for students to voice, describe, use, and build from their experiences.

I started asking myself what might change if instead of defending my intentions, I accepted responsibility for the outcomes, and I moved toward **immersion/emersion.** Every once in a while, I thought I could start to see something that looked like systemic and institutionalized racism, but then my white privilege would show up and make it invisible again. I spent a lot of time squinting to see what was right in front of me. When I could see it, I felt afraid and daunted by how huge and complex racism is. I had moments of being afraid to speak up for fear of saying the wrong thing, but mostly I feared making things worse. After the murder of Trayvon Martin, a Black woman friend asked me what I was going to do to keep her Black son safe. This conversation, and others like it, made me realize that my fear of speaking up was not valid in the face of the fear that my friend faces every day for her family.

Autonomy still feels aspirational; the more I know, the more I understand how much I don't know. I try to stare at those feelings of superiority that still arrive and to acknowledge them, because the more I try to deny them, the bigger they get. I have been able to take back the parts of myself that I had disassociated from before, and now nothing makes me feel better after a hard day than watching a good British costume drama. I feel better able to feel compassion for white people, even when they frustrate me, including myself.

Elizabeth's Story

I grew up in Silicon Valley as it was coming into being, and most everyone looked, talked, and sounded like me. I was raised in an Italian and Irish–Catholic family, and both sides of my family immigrated to the United States around the turn of the century. I was very aware of my ethnic identity because my grandparents spoke only Italian, and my mom often talked about her grandmother from Ireland. But we never talked about being *white*. And while my hometown was majority white, the surrounding towns were filled with People of Color. So, I have memories of talking about the race of others, just not my own. But those observations of racial identity were generally made in hushed tones from my parents—a very clear message that I was not to talk about race. I was able to stay in the **contact** stage for a long time, and any time I encountered what I now know to be racism, I was able to come up with a different logical explanation for why it was not about race.

When I first started teaching many years later, I joined a school midway through the year and was asked to take over a literature class that had erupted a few days before I started because of the use of a racial slur in a story by William Faulkner. The previous teacher had been challenged by the African American students in the class, who were tired of reading the N-word in their classes. They had heard the "rationale" and explanations, and they said they were sick of having to endure the racism in their classes with their predominantly white peers and teachers.

I remember thinking, why can't they see the argument for teaching that particular story? Surely, we were not racist for teaching it, and Faulkner was simply using the term he had heard. What was the problem, and why were these young people so upset? And then I realized it was the very first conversation I had ever had with African American students on the subject of race. This was a textbook moment from Helms's (2019) work, my **contact** stage moment in which I was still unaware of my whiteness and was asserting my worldview as "normal."

The following school year, I had a very different experience teaching an Ethnic Voices class at another school. The class was split evenly along racial lines: eight white students and eight Students of Color. What I didn't realize was that I tipped the balance; my whiteness counted. The Students of Color were experiencing many different levels of racism, and I was having a very difficult time managing the class. I was in way over my head. About six weeks into the term, the eight Students of Color showed up at my desk. They told me they had decided to drop the class, and they were willing to get an F and risk losing college acceptances because the racism they were experiencing was intolerable. Because I had not come to terms with my identity, the class was facing its own crisis. They looked at me intently and asked what I could do. What could I do? I told the students I would find a way to make it better. I asked them to give me two weeks, and they agreed. Then I cried for three days, signaling a shift to the **disintegration** stage. Suddenly, I was aware that racism had something to do with me, and I was awash in feelings of guilt and shame.

Once I realized that I needed to figure out what being a white woman meant for me, I began to look for some narratives that might help my own exploration. Ruth Frankenberg's (1993) study of 40 white women significantly impacted my understanding of whiteness (see Introduction for definition). So, I wasn't just "Elizabeth." I was *raced*, and that positionality meant something—it affected what and whom I noticed and what I didn't. It was also the beginning of a racial group membership for me. And it was here that I toggled between Helms's (2019) **reintegration** and **pseudoindependence** stages. I was battling my own feelings of guilt and shame and often was angry that to be white was to be presumed guilty of racism. I was still bristling at the fact that I may be a part of the problem. I was also in the midst of a huge intellectual transformation, consuming every text about race and racism that I could.

Another indicator of my status in the **pseudoindependence** phase was my desire to work *only* with People of Color. I remember being so mad at other white people. I call this my "I'm gonna hit you over the head with a frying pan" stage. Whack! I was going to make sure every white person understood racism and white privilege. I was done with all the foolishness. I was going to clean up this racism mess once and for all! Now we call this the "smartest white person in the room" moment, and I was great at it. Perhaps most importantly, it is a space filled with arrogance. I remember thinking, "I can't believe people haven't figured out how to end racism yet." The fact that I could now see racism was quickly processed as "What's wrong with the rest of y'all?" Here is white supremacy at perhaps one of its most effective moments: Because I now see something, I must have discovered it. And I, alone, will remedy it.

In 2001, I had my first antiracist white affinity group experience, and it helped to move me toward the **immersion/emersion** phase. Until then, all of the dialogue was in my head, happening as I read books and cited research. To be in a space with other white people talking about our identity was a profound shift that helped me to see how much I had to gain from other white people. I had relied on the stories of People of Color to teach me about racism. But this was the first time I could see my role and how I had been carefully reenacting my part in a play, written well before my time. Other white people had felt and noticed the same things as me; I was not unique and special. And together we could be way more effective.

Dipping my toe into the **autonomy** phase helped to clarify why white people need to talk to other white people. I started antiracist white affinity groups at my school, and every year we had to fight for it to happen. It was the Staff of Color who supported the white affinity space, often saying, "Yes, PLEASE, go talk with your people." It helped me really see racism as a *system*, not just a dynamic of "good" and "bad" white people. Every year, white people would fight the existence of these groups. They would argue with vague and nebulous statements, always about this "feeling" they had, which I now understand was their profound discomfort. They seemed so convinced, and in my head, I started to question the program. That's how white collusion with racism works—white folks are really good at getting other white folks to stay in line and support the status quo and doing it all with a calm tone of voice and positive facial expression. I could start to see how these white colleagues really believed what they were saying. There was no way they were complicit, and their feedback to me was genuine. I could now recognize myself in them. And that empathy helps me have more compassion and resolution. I'm grateful for these fleeting moments of autonomy, when I feel like I am part of an antiracist community where our whiteness can be recognized, interrogated, and used to fight racism and diminish the harm to People of Color. I struggle to fight the judgement that can creep in, and I strive to stay as humble as I can while also holding myself and others accountable.

———

As you can see, there are some common threads between our two stories and some unique experiences that have guided our ways into racial awareness. If this were prescriptive, we would all be able to see the clear way forward, but it is not. Ultimately, the work of locating yourself within white identity and how you have been shaped by your race is yours to do and understand. We want to offer encouragement to engage in this process, as we both feel the grounding that comes with a clearer reflection of ourselves. There is an ease that comes in not having to tie ourselves into knots to avoid knowing certain things about ourselves. There is encouragement in no longer being paralyzed by shame and guilt. There is comfort in knowing our strengths and in being able to name and nurture the parts of ourselves that need continued growth and support. There is relief in causing less harm to the People of Color in our lives. There is joy in defogging the mirror.

Our Working Assumptions and Actions

To help us better see how our identity shows up in our teaching, we created a series of statements to help keep us focused on our antiracist work. This list was inspired by Dr. Beverly Daniel Tatum's working assumptions (1992) that she used to begin all of her courses on racial identity development. We have found them helpful as guideposts for the work we strive to do, and they serve as an important foundation for why we founded the Teaching While White project. We have also included a list of actions that help us hold ourselves accountable for our antiracist work and ensure that it is observable.

- Privilege and prejudice are two sides of the same coin; as I am elevated, someone else is marginalized or oppressed.
- It is critical to distinguish between prejudice and racism: racism = prejudice + power + privilege.
- I will never see the world through the eyes of a Person of Color; my attempts to make comparisons of exclusion will never be on par with what People of Color might face in certain contexts.
- As a woman, I can relate to gender inequality. In many ways, oppression cuts across social identifiers, but experiences of oppression can be different and need to be recognized.
- My white identity includes white privilege as an aspect of my whiteness. It is a part of what it means to be white, and I must be willing to accept this reality.
- Solidarity does not mean everyone thinks alike; multiracial solidarity is geared toward points of intersection, not false universalism or false unity (McLaren, 2014).
- I do not expect People of Color to thank me or to acknowledge my

antiracist work. I consider it my moral and professional responsibility and will not look for validation from People of Color.

- Individual accountability is what changes cultures; the way I see myself is intimately connected to the way I see others. If I don't understand what it means to be white, how can I ever hope to understand another colleague or student?
- If I am called a racist, it is not the end of the conversation. It is the beginning.
- I recognize that there will be what Enid Lee calls "slippage" in my work, meaning that sometimes I will make mistakes in the process of learning how to dismantle racism. Yet I know I must pick myself up and keep going, and it will be easier each time.
- If I begin to feel complacent, thinking that I have "done" antiracism, or the need to list my credentials, then I know I still have a lot of work to do.

Based on the above assumptions, these are my actions:

- Explore my own whiteness; become firmly rooted and aware of my own racial/ethnic identity; think about what it means to be white in my school.
- See myself as racially diverse; make sure that "multicultural" is not synonymous with "other than white."
- Distinguish between individual and group identity.
- Understand the social, political, and historical role of teaching:
  - I will teach the way I was taught unless I learn another way.
  - Teachers are not neutral; teaching strategies and methods are not objective.
  - We all speak from a particular standpoint based on our experiences.
  - There is no essential, observable, single truth; rather, there are multiple truths.
  - Everything is not relative, but rather we recognize that cognition—the way we think and learn—is dependent on experience and context.
- Understand and implement antiracist teaching strategies; design

a curriculum that is explicitly antiracist; be committed to raising issues of identity development in my classroom.

- Learn the distinction between speaking for someone and speaking with someone; be committed to dialogue, as opposed to discussion, when appropriate.
- Recognize the difference between intentions and outcomes:

   Schools are full of people "who without intending to create racial hurdles or hostility, manage to create a fair amount of both. That they cannot see what they have done is due partly to the fact that they meant no harm and partly to a disinclination to examine whether the assumptions they hold dear are in accord with reality." (Cose, 1994)

- Practice "distinguishing" (Carter & Denevi, 2006) behavior: interrupting prejudice and/or racism, advocating for social justice, using my privilege to dismantle systems of oppression.

ACTIVITY: WHAT IS YOUR "WHY"?

Self-awareness and clarity of purpose are essential to sustaining our commitment when we operate in a culture that encourages us, at every turn, to do nothing. When we know **why** we are invested in being actively antiracist and have clarity about **what** we are moving toward, we can withstand bouts of uncertainty, self-doubt, and criticism. Your answers to the following questions will be dynamic, and it may take several iterations before you land on one statement that resonates and inspires you. It may also be that a statement works for a time and then may plateau, requiring you to reimagine and redraft your statement of purpose.

You have to have this sense of faith that what you're moving toward is already done. It's already happened. It's the power to believe that you can see, that you visualize, that sense of community, that sense of family, that sense of one house. If you visualize it, if you can even have faith that it's there for you, it is already there.

—John Lewis, "On Being With Krista Tippett," July 5, 2016

What Is Your "Why"?

Why are you invested in working toward being more antiracist? What is the cost of racism for you personally? What have you let go of and what new behaviors will you embrace? What will you gain from actively challenging racism?

CHAPTER 3

Analyzing How Whiteness Operates as a System in Our Schools

Previously, we described how our white racial consciousness develops over time and in various contexts. We can see and name how our identity is impacted by racism and how we can develop a positive racial identity that is not based on superiority, but in solidarity with communities that are fighting racism. In this chapter we want to delineate some of the ways that racism and white supremacy show up in schools. We want to illustrate the contours of how whiteness often operates as unnamed, unmarked, and it passes for "normal" not only for individuals, but also for educational institutions.

Similar to the way many white people struggle with "I'm racist" versus "I'm *not* racist," institutions can be limited in their perspective of what it means to be antiracist. They can struggle to really see where and how racism may be operating and often see only the ends of the spectrum and none of the points in between. Thus, we want to offer Helms's (2019) stages as a jumping off point to locate particular institutional behaviors that can be observed, named, and used as indicators of where an educational institution needs to direct its antiracist efforts. The focus on behavior also helps us to assess and evaluate our efforts to make institutions less racist. In education, we value skills we can measure, and so our efforts to challenge racism need to include a similar delineation of skills that can be observed, evaluated, and refined over time.

Your School Is Already Raced:
Predominantly White Institutions

We know that individuals come to understand their racial identity via experiences over time. Schools, too, need to understand and grapple with their racial identity as institutions. They have their own *collective* racial identity, which will impact policies and procedures, curricular initiatives, recruitment and retention efforts, and other systemic issues. We focus here on predominantly white educational institutions (PWIs), whose histories and ideologies center whiteness as the dominant culture. Most existing schools, colleges, and universities in this country were created by and for white people, apart from the few institutions created to serve People of Color specifically, such as historically Black colleges and universities (HBCUs). Most educational power structures reflect that history, even institutions with a higher percentage of racial diversity.

We use Dr. Helms's (2019) stages that we looked at in Chapter 1 and apply them to various functions of institutional practices and cultures. By understanding how each status operates, we are better positioned to name and subvert racism across an institution. Just as it is rare for individual white people to be solely in one racial status, one aspect of a school can be in one stage while another might be in a different stage. And in the wake of some racial crisis, an institution might move swiftly into a different status. Change requires an unflinching look at the places our behavior may not align with our beliefs, and educational institutions need to be clear about the gaps between espoused beliefs in racial equity and the realities on campus. When applied more broadly to PWIs, the stages of racial identity development can point to inconsistencies and areas for strategic antiracist interventions. The following are examples as well as "snapshots" of institutional moments to illuminate how racism is operating and places where the status quo can be disrupted.

Institutional Statuses and Snapshots

Contact

Perhaps as a byproduct or a willful hanging on of racial segregation in the United States, many schools operate in the contact phase, thinking of themselves as "just normal." They function in a kind of racial isolation and operate as "colorblind." They do not see or name race and especially do not acknowledge whiteness. They espouse a strong belief in school success as a meritocracy and believe any child who tries hard enough will succeed. They advocate for universal ways of being that everyone in the school community should believe in and adopt, with tangible consequence for those who do not go along with the program. Institutions that are primarily in the contact stage believe that racism is really not an issue. If it was, that was in the past, and for the most part was resolved in the civil rights era. Racism is only viewed as or acknowledged as a few individual acts of unkindness or meanness, but certainly nothing that is pervasive or institution-wide.

For example, an institution might demonstrate their contact status by:

- actively supporting "gifted and talented" programs as reflective of innate academic ability or IQ;
- pervasive and unchallenged tracking by achievement level, which is seen as just the way to teach;
- policy or custom, such as challenging and/or banning signs like "Black Lives Matter" for being discriminatory;
- not discussing/acknowledging the history of the institution if it was connected to injustice in the past (e.g., was a white-flight school during the civil rights movement or at some point would not admit African American students);
- not tracking and/or analyzing achievement and discipline data by race;
- maintaining a curriculum that follows an overwhelming pattern of the "Western tradition," with lots of references to "canonical" texts; or

- emphasizing similarity and unity and demonstrating an unwillingness to discuss what is seen as "divisive."

Contact Snapshot

There is a general feeling that "we" are all one big happy family, a caring and dedicated staff who love all the children. No racist incidents or issues are discussed, making vague references to "celebrating diversity." The third grade curriculum on immigration is a reenactment of the Ellis Island experience, and all children will dress up as an ancestor who came to the United States via its inspection station. The fact that almost all children in the gifted and talented program are white is not seen as any kind of issue but rather reinforces what the faculty observe on a daily basis—especially since there may be a few exceptional Students of Color in the program.

Disintegration

Institutions are usually pushed into disintegration when some information that is difficult to refute comes forward that directly contradicts the institutional belief that it is a "happy family" that does not see color, only people. Usually, it requires a group of Faculty, Students, or Parents of Color to come forward and identify some area of gross inequality, such as looking at grades, discipline stats, and/or graduation rates disaggregated by race. We also saw this with "Black@" when Black students created Instagram accounts as a place to come forward and describe the racist incidents they experienced at independent schools, colleges, and universities across the country. These types of events illuminate the discrepancy between the perception of the leadership of an institution and those who have been marginalized by it. When confronted in this way, the typical first response is anger and denial. This often takes the form of disputing the validity of the data or questioning, "Is this really about race?" When contradictory data or testimony is impossible to reason away, institutions often respond with guilt and shame. As institutions start to become conscious of the ways they advantage white people, they attempt to manage their feelings of disequilibrium and outrage. They can be quickly overwhelmed by the enormity of the problem and spin, trying to figure out where to start, which leads to paralysis.

For example, an educational institution might demonstrate their disintegration status by:

- sponsoring diversity festivals or multicultural nights that celebrate our differences under the umbrella of the "human family" in response to this new awareness of racial differences;
- one department adding a book about a racially underrepresented group that is written by a white author or including a "multicultural unit" without changing any other aspect of the curriculum or instruction;
- standing by statements that decry, "This is not who we are!" in the face of emerging racial disparities;
- implementing community/service-learning trips to "help" those "in need";
- ending a faculty meeting with great upset and emotion after Faculty of Color share their experiences of racist incidents on campus; or
- campus leaders reaching out to a few Students of Color or Alumni of Color to learn about their experiences.

Disintegration Snapshot

A school receives data that shows that there is a wide "achievement gap" for Black boys. The principal of the school, believing this is a self-esteem issue and not symptomatic of a larger issue, instructs all the faculty to pick one Black boy they teach and write them a letter of encouragement.

Reintegration

Reintegration is potentially the most dangerous status for an institution. Feelings of guilt and anxiety shift to hostility and anger toward those who are marginalized, as it is easier to avoid issues of racism rather than address them, which may cause a struggle to redefine the institution. In response to "Black@," there are now Instagram posts to "Woke@" that challenge antiracist efforts as going too far and accusing institutions of discriminating against white people, citing "the bias in antibias" education. Schools in this stage often seek out data and information that places blame on People of Color in an attempt to absolve the institution of responsibility, opting to try to fix kids instead of the systems that fail them. This reinforces the underlying (often unconscious) belief in white intellectual and academic superiority.

Here are some examples of how an educational institution might demonstrate their reintegration status:

- Community Members of Color who challenge racist institutional culture may be questioned as to why they want to be at the institution if they dislike it so much.
- White staff and faculty defend their intentions and support each other in not noticing or acknowledging racial harm when it is observed or reported.
- In response to racial disparities and requests for accommodations, educators make statements like, "We can't make everyone happy, so we need to just stick to what we know and get back to basics."
- When confronted with opportunities or requests for change to the status quo that would address racial disparities, the institution responds with, "We just don't have the resources, time, or money to make such drastic changes."
- A disproportionate number of Students of Color are brought forward at "kids of concern" meetings, are referred for testing and special education, and are subjected to disciplinary actions.
- White faculty and staff comment on how Students and Families of Color should be more grateful for all the support, opportunities, and extra attention they receive.
- Substantially fewer Faculty and Staff of Color are hired, retained, or tenured than white faculty and staff. Hiring committees raise questions of "fit" or qualification regarding Candidates of Color.
- Parents of Color who come forward with any complaint are labeled angry, unreasonable, or mentally unstable.
- Students are suspended, expelled, or counseled out as a result of their lack of ability, unaccepted behavior, and/or complaints about racist institutional policies.

Reintegration Snapshot

A school sends several faculty members to a racial diversity conference for professional development. The decision to send teachers stemmed from a growing awareness of racial incidents happening on campus. Once faculty returned to campus, the administration declared that those who attended the conference would not be allowed to wear the t-shirts they had received there that said "Check your privilege" on them. Leadership decided that the statement was making the white students uncomfortable.

Pseudoindependence

As institutions start to actively try to dismantle systems that reinforce white superiority, they set about working to diversify the school community and curriculum. With a growing sense of urgency, leadership seeks to fix problems, often rushing to find answers without consulting with those who are most impacted by their decisions. Sometimes this is because they have not considered the value of other perspectives. Other times they may be demonstrating the lingering embedded belief in white superiority. Paradoxically, institutions often solicit advice and testimony from People of Color but still act in ways that belie their feedback. Institutions at this stage also act as white saviors and maintain a host/guest mentality by offering more programming to support "at risk" students, faculty, or families. Having heard that they cannot expect or rely on People of Color to teach them about racism, white leaders will continue to make decisions that do not take into account the impact on People of Color, saying they did not want to place undue or additional stress on the few Faculty of Color.

For example, an educational institution might demonstrate their pseudoindependence status by:

- having book clubs that serve as a primary catalyst for racial awareness and that support intellectual responses to understanding how racism operates;
- firing or placing on leave white educators who do or say racist things instead of offering support and training in order to distance themselves from that behavior;

- providing remedial, credit recovery, and/or summer "bridge" programs that seek to address student "deficits" so they can be more ready, able, etc.;
- offering one or two trainings on how to address racism (box checked);
- using an additive approach to curriculum that still centers white Western traditions/canon, while adding in a few People of Color in particular fields, and typically representing People of Color as either exceptions or victims of oppression;
- creating affinity groups for People of Color only, continuing to believe that white people don't have a race or that it isn't their place to comment on such matters; or
- enabling white staff who actively spot *other* white people as racist and feel the need to expose the ignorance of others, including students, whom they think should "know better," in their efforts to show their commitment to challenging racism.

Pseudoindependence Snapshot

It has been brought to the school's attention that the soccer team has been using the N-word on the field and during games. They want to do what is right and decide to punish the team and require that they go to a training on the history of that word. During the training, it becomes clear that none of the students have had a conversation about this word and its impact with an adult before, though they all describe seeing it in English and history texts they had been required to read.

Immersion/Emersion

Educational institutions in the immersion/emersion stage acknowledge their status as a predominantly white institution and continually reflect on how race affects experiences, policies, and procedures. They can recognize, name, and understand how white dominant culture influences the institution and how racism impacts the culture and climate. They seek and develop positive role models for institutional climate and culture that are not based in white superiority, but in antiracism. These institutions recognize the inherent value of racial diversity on campus and how nurturing pluralism supports academic and social growth for everyone. Immersion/emersion stage institutions explore the role of white educators in dismantling racism, moving away from relying on Educators of Color to make change.

For example, an educational institution might demonstrate their immersion/emersion status by:

- supporting racial affinity groups for both People of Color and antiracist whites;
- moving from blaming a particular person to seeing how systems support inequity, especially in regard to disciplinary practices;
- having curricular audits to see how race manifests across a particular discipline or grade level;
- analyzing assessment practices and how racial inequity is operating via grading policies, tracking, feedback, etc.; or
- taking responsibility for racial harm and acknowledging the consequences of racial inequity.

Immersion/Emersion Snapshot

Departments review how their grading and assessment practices may be influenced by expectations, bias, and stereotypes. They work together to develop detailed rubrics that clearly identify expectations of assignments so students can see exactly why they received a particular grade. They record student conferences to see if the quality of their feedback changes based on race. For example, do white teachers give more detailed and specific feedback to white students than to Students of Color?

Autonomy

Educational institutions in the autonomy stage acknowledge white supremacy as a system that affects every aspect of the institution and make a sustained and transparent commitment to racial equity. That belief is explicit and embedded in the institution's mission, values, and daily operations. White educators are charged with and skilled in dismantling racism. Leadership actively seeks and incorporates feedback on antiracist work, especially from Community Members of Color. The institution nurtures multiracial solidarity and affirms the value of a spectrum of racial and ethnic identities and cultures, including ways of knowing, demonstrations of knowledge, and modes of communication. Autonomous institutions recognize that challenging racism is an ongoing process and demonstrate a determination to do better, understanding that there is not a box to check nor an arrival point. They foster institutional humility in their constant pursuit of greater racial literacy, evaluation of progress, and accountability.

Here are some examples of an educational institution demonstrating autonomy status:

- Race does not predict academic outcomes, graduation rates, or disciplinary processes.
- Faculty and staff reflect the racial diversity of the student body; People of Color are significantly represented across leadership roles and departments.
- All departments consistently collect, disaggregate, and review data by race, looking for patterns to disrupt.
- Curricula explicitly address issues of identity, difference, and power across grade levels and disciplines.
- They include racial literacy as a part of their performance evaluations and feedback cycles.
- White people at the institution consistently engage other white people on topics of racial difference, stereotypes, prejudice, and racism.
- Accountability and assessment measures are pervasive and rely on the stakeholders who are most impacted to determine the success of initiatives or policies.

Autonomy Snapshot

As part of the math curriculum, students research the impact of the area's minimum wage on particular racial and ethnic groups. Faculty are committed to looking at the intersectionality of race and class and systematically ask all students to explore their own racial identity. Depending on the grade level, students research statistics and compare data from different sources. Younger learners look at a menu from a local restaurant to see if they could afford to go out to eat if they had to live on minimum wage. Older learners analyze disproportionate effects and the cost of wage inequality by race. Students are asked to interview local business people and community members and compare their findings. Students are also asked to reach out to their local representatives to learn about the state government's role in eliminating income inequality by race and supporting living wages for all.

Now That We Know, What Can We Do?

Predominantly white institutions are made up of white people navigating their racial identity in the context of a larger institution that is also impacted by race and racism via its mission, policies, and procedures. Our roles and responsibilities are in the interplay between our positionality and the institutions we serve. Thus, we need not only a path through our own personal development, but also a way to measure how institutions can get better at challenging racism. By noticing where a school's practices fall among the various stages of abandoning racism to adopting antiracism, we can meet an institution where it is and shift aspects of culture in discernable ways. We can then track over time the effectiveness of our efforts and avoid predictable traps and detours. As noted in Chapter 2, just as individuals can occupy multiple stages at once, an institution can find itself in several stages as well. For example, one department may be in a very different stage from another. Finally, we often note that we can *tell* a school what to do to be less racist, but the institution must be willing and able to see, name, and enact different practices according to its own mission and values. We hope the articulation of these institutional characteristics can serve as a blueprint or map of the terrain educational institutions need to cover. The following chapters will identify particular aspects of school operations and constituent groups that can be mobilized to enact strategic change.

ACTIVITY: THE ELEVATOR PITCH

Awareness and clarity of purpose are essential to sustaining commitment. Why do you, as an educational institution, want to embark on or support greater equity? Does everyone within the community have a clear understanding of why the institution is doing this work? Understanding that change can be difficult for some. Does everyone have a clear understanding of the gains that will be made, and can they articulate them in the face of resistance? Are those gains and goals clearly stated by the institution?

To develop your "pitch," try this activity with your team:

Imagine that you are standing outside the main office one day after school. A white parent you have met once before approaches you and asks about the school's diversity and equity work. They note that there have been a lot of messages lately about the need to talk more about race at school. But this parent is unclear why their kid needs to talk about race, especially at such a young age. You are about to go to the faculty meeting and have just a few minutes to make a cogent argument for this parent. What would you say? Practice with a partner about what racial justice means to you and your institution. Why do you do it? What do you think the benefits are? Be sure to set a timer to see if you can get your "elevator pitch" conveyed in 2 minutes or less.

PART II

STEPS
FOR ACTION
—
ANTIRACIST STRATEGIES
FOR EDUCATIONAL
COMMUNITIES

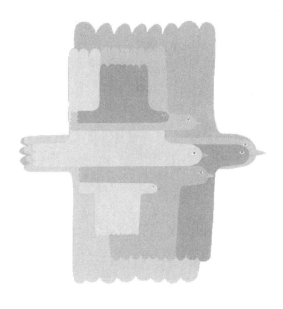

CHAPTER 4

Locating Ourselves Within Whiteness

As we described earlier, foggy mirrors are distortions of racial reality. When we can recognize and articulate all the ways that being white has created our perspective and shaped our experiences as white teachers, we help wipe the mirrors clean and provide truer reflections for ourselves and our students. When both white students and teachers can draw on that racial awareness, we start to narrow the space where misinformation, isolation, and dominance thrive.

Growing this self-awareness and racial consciousness is at the root of all we do as antiracist educators because without it, even with the best intentions and the best curriculum, we can still cause harm. For example, a white teacher decides to teach a Black Lives Matter unit through film. The teacher wants the white kids in his class to "get out of their bubble" and feels it is his responsibility to "wake them up" by listing how many Black people have been killed by police. The teacher also believes that his one Black student in the class will experience this unit as affirming, but never checks in with that student. The white teacher and white students discuss the films as an intellectual exercise while the one Black student experiences, in real time, racial stress and trauma. The unit is meticulously planned and developed with the admirable intentions of addressing current events and teaching about racism explicitly. However, the teacher never considered the impact of his own racial identity, the racial make-up of the class, or the implicit messages that could reinforce stereotypes of People of Color as victims only and white people as violent oppressors only. Additionally, the teacher positioned himself as a white savior and encouraged his students to do the same by emphasizing the need for white people to get involved for this issue to be taken seriously.

What if instead. . .

- The teacher invited the Black student into a conversation prior to teaching the unit?
- The curriculum already had representation of how Black people have resisted oppression and included other contributions and moments of joy for People of Color?
- The teacher made his whiteness explicit, acknowledging his racial blind spots and/or partnered with a Black teacher, parent, or community member to teach the unit?
- He taught about the white savior narrative explicitly and encouraged students to be on the lookout for ways the media might be embedding it in their reporting of racial uprisings?

There are many ways this unit could have been taught differently and had the impact he intended. But the teacher would have needed greater racial awareness to think of these ideas. Too often, white teachers defer to and rely on Teachers of Color to bring up racial topics and to point out any of our missteps, further replicating the pattern of thinking that there is no issue unless those who are most marginalized by race choose to speak up. We need to do our own homework. This chapter focuses on the many ways that white people can work together to support their racial identity development and help each other see how white supremacy may be operating.

Learning From Other White People

When more white people can notice and name racially problematic moments or practices, it takes some of the burden off People of Color to bring issues forward. It also means more people, sitting at more tables, on more committees, with different spheres of influence, are interrupting the status quo and contributing to antiracist change. We have spent a significant amount of time setting up and facilitating informal and formal white antiracist affinity groups for educators. Of all the work we do in schools, some of the biggest shifts in school culture that we have seen stemmed from these kinds of accountability spaces.

These groups can take many forms. Sometimes the group is a couple white teachers working together on a grade-level team. White members of a department may work together to notice how their racial identity impacts their work in their particular subject matter. Given that many schools have professional learning communities (PLCs), white teachers could set up a PLC to look at their racial socialization and how it affects their assessment practices or curriculum choices. Because of the interplay between white individuals and predominantly white institutions, we strongly encourage participants to spend the bulk of the time doing self-reflection to understand all the ways whiteness has shaped their experience and perspective and how it continues to influence how they interact in the world. The temptation is to start fixing other people and situations. As we illustrated in the opening scenario, white people often replicate and enforce inequitable systems when they do not deepen their racial consciousness.

There are many articles and books that can be used as an anchor for meetings, as long as the conversation is not just intellectual. We often use Shelly Tochluk's (2010) book *Witnessing Whiteness*, which comes with the added benefit of online activities for each chapter. *Waking Up White*, by Debby Irving (2014), is another useful resource that has questions for discussion after each chapter. *Me and White Supremacy*, by Layla Saad (2020), provides interactive prompts and journaling. No matter the vehicle, the goal is to grow racial consciousness so that we can teach and live in greater racial awareness and with alignment between our stated beliefs and our actions. What follows are some specific areas and activities that we have found useful in this process.

Colluding With White Talk

Part of being able to interrupt racism is the ability to recognize it while it is happening, and white people can really help each other to see how we often collude with white supremacy when we either don't see or don't speak up in certain situations. Alice McIntyre (1997) describes the coded ways white people talk about race as "white talk." It is a way for white people to distance themselves from the difficult task of engaging in an exploration and critique of whiteness and racism. White talk manifests itself as the uncritical acceptance of biased comments via avoidance, counterarguments, interruption, silence, and/or colluding with each other to make it very difficult to discuss patterns of white behavior. By identifying white talk, we can recognize the price whites pay for this kind of collusion and begin to see how privilege is maintained.

One of the main forms of white talk is minimization, signaling that achievement depends on personal ability and that racism is not in fact prevalent. Another manifestation is defensiveness disguised as disclaimers such as, "I'm not racist. I love all my students. Why does it always have to be about race? I went to a workshop on white privilege." Another insidious form of avoidance is "if only" statements, declarations that set conditions on one's commitment to racial justice: "If only People of Color weren't so angry. If only People of Color would tell us when something is a problem."

Recently, we were working with a group of white educators who had hit a roadblock in their antiracist work. They were feeling their stress levels increase and were worried about their relationships with Colleagues of Color. A few mentioned that sometimes People of Color seemed to be telling them about something that was racist, but they weren't very specific. They alluded to some behavior that wasn't appropriate. They didn't directly say what happened, and white colleagues were left wondering, "Are they talking about me? I really want to know. Why won't they tell us?" This is an important example of "white talk": If only People of Color would. . .

We asked the group, "Given that you are all often scared to confront each other or to ask questions when race comes up, what would it mean for a Person of Color to offer feedback? Might they be watching your pattern? If you all are judging each other, what might you do to a Person of Color who names racism?" It was a critical reflection moment that stopped the "if only" comment in its tracks and redirected the conversation back to where it needed to be: on the behavior of the white people.

When we hear people using forms white talk and we are silent, we are colluding with racism. We may believe our silence in these moments is neutral, respectful, or even polite. Yet, we are prioritizing our own comfort and the comfort of other white people. It is a choice. Most often, what is at stake for white people when we interrupt are the risks of being disliked, engaging in a conflict, ruining a family gathering, being perceived as a troublemaker, or being perceived as thinking we are better than others. At times there are real consequences, such as a relationship ending or a job being at stake, but usually we are avoiding some form of social discomfort, often something to do with our ego. But what is at stake if we *don't* interrupt racist comments and behaviors? We are allowing and signing off on harm to People of Color, supporting the status quo, not living the values we espouse, and jeopardizing our integrity.

Below is a scenario to practice your skills for interrupting white talk, but the format can easily be applied to situations from your own school community. It is designed for the participation of white people to practice with their white colleagues. In this format, there are three roles, and we recommend playing through three scenarios so everyone can play each role once. The Mistake-Maker is the person who says or does something racially problematic. The Interrupter is the person who is practicing not letting racist moments go uninterrogated. The Listener is there to observe and to reflect any strategies that worked well and any missed opportunities. This kind of critical feedback is also a valuable skill to develop.

The objective is to keep the Mistake-Maker engaged and wanting to know more. It is tempting to want to just talk through the scenario and guess at what you might say or do, but it is exponentially more effective to actually role-play, even for just a few minutes. When we put ourselves in the situation and have to practice an actual response and engage in dialogue, we have the opportunity to work through some of the awkwardness and discomfort while not in the heat of a real moment. This creates a kind of "muscle memory" so that the next time you find yourself in a racially stressful situation, you have a plan of action. After the role-play, there are guiding questions for the trio to discuss.

ACTIVITY: INTERRUPTING ROLE PLAY

Mistake-Maker: You have been required to do a summer read of a book about white privilege. You hate the word "privilege" and wonder why the author can't just use a different term. You didn't grow up with privilege; in fact, you grew up quite poor. You are not saying that there isn't racism, but you dislike the way the author writes about the topic and think that there must be a better book, in which the author doesn't make so many presumptions about how white people grew up.

Interrupter: How will you address the different concerns that you hear? How can you help your colleague see why it is important for faculty to read this book?

Listener: What stood out to you in both people's arguments? Did the Interrupter address the root issue? How or how not? Can you think of anything to add to clarify why what the Mistake-Maker said was problematic?

Discussion Questions:
- What are the assumptions and root issues within this scenario?
- What is at stake if this moment goes uninterrupted?
- Given your identity, and your sphere of influence, how might you interrupt?
- Are there any actions that can be taken as a preventative measure so it doesn't happen again?

It is useful to notice strategies that could work across a range of scenarios. For example, are there ways of sharing genuine curiosity and asking questions of the Mistake-Maker to better understand their perspective? As the Interrupter, were you able to speak about your own mistakes and experiences from a place of humility that invited more discussion? It is also important to notice whether it feels easier to interrupt one person than another. Are you more comfortable bringing things to the attention of colleagues than to a supervisor or a parent? And is this easier to do with students than with adults? Can you think of other scenarios that might be useful to practice?

Ultimately, when working toward antiracism, it is our job to stand shoulder to shoulder with other white people even when they make mistakes. We need more white people fighting for racial justice, and we need to invite them in through any conversation we can.

White Antiracist Affinity Groups for Teachers

If you are looking for a more organized way to develop your antiracist practice, you can explore the development of a white racial affinity group, sometimes referred to as a caucus or resource group. Different from clubs or interest groups, affinity groups bring together people with similar backgrounds or identities. Although members of the group share a common identity of being white, it does not mean that everyone in that group shares the *exact* same experiences. Rather, participants recognize that their whiteness affects the way they move through the world and the way the world sees them. The goals of white antiracist affinity groups are:

1. to develop a positive racial identity that is not based in superiority, saviorism, or guilt/shame, but in the recognition of our shared racialized experiences;
2. to gain a sense of our antiracist group membership and collective impact; and
3. to build the skills necessary for recognizing how racism operates in order to take action both personally and systemically.

White teachers need a space where they can develop and practice what it looks, sounds, and feels like to interrupt business as usual. They can process their racial stress, ask questions, practice how to interrupt white supremacy with other white people, and practice how to hold each other accountable for the ways we reinforce and recreate racism. And we can do it without taxing People of Color in the process. These meetings can often allay fears, helping participants understand the importance of acknowledging their racial group membership as antiracists. Many say they feel uncomfortable identifying as "white" because when they hear the term, they just think "racist." And when we are operating from a collective sense of shame, it makes it very difficult to work together or with People of Color. If we can't accept our own difference, it's impossible to accept someone else's. When we have a strong sense of our racial identity along with the skills to challenge racism, we can intentionally create productive antiracist teaching/learning environments in principled partnerships with People of Color.

White antiracist affinity groups do not take the place of cross-racial dialogue. Because most white people have not *had* to think about race and racism, we are typically not practiced at understanding or describing how our race has impacted our lives. It is akin to trying to discuss algebra when many people in the room only understand addition. If I, as a white person, have spent most of my life not thinking about my race, I have a kind of arrested development. So if I'm talking with someone who has been thinking about their race for their entire life, we are not going to be on the same page. These conversations can come at a great cost to People of Color, as they are often being asked to show and prove why their race matters. These conversations can also cause white people to feel frustrated and ultimately to disengage altogether because they have no idea that their race matters. Affinity groups can be a place to do some of the catch-up work that allows for more productive cross-racial conversations.

Whenever possible, we recommend having an experienced white facilitator to create the agenda and/or syllabus for the meetings, which we suggest happen at least once a month. The content builds over time, and you want to keep the momentum going. A facilitator can ensure you don't get stuck in a particular stage of development. For example, the initial and sometimes sudden awakening to racism as a system can paralyze white participants who are overwhelmed by the magnitude of the problem. Someone with a larger context can help shift participants out of their anxiousness and into a broader focus. Also, a facilitator who is not part of the school community will be outside the power dynamics that may be present in the room and can keep the group on task. Though there is often pushback regarding the cost of hiring a facilitator for affinity groups, when launching any other initiative, a new website platform for example, schools typically find the necessary funds.

Anticipating and Meeting Resistance

So why meet just with white people? Isn't that segregation? Even if you don't believe this is segregation, you will most certainly have to answer this question if you chose to create or participate in white antiracist affinity groups. Though it often goes unobserved, it is common for there to be meetings and rooms that are populated with white people only. However, the moment it is an *intentionally* white group with the purpose of talking about race, it is suddenly seen as racist or, at the very least, separatist. Historically, and in the not-so-distant past, the only time white people gathered with an intention to talk about race was to ally themselves around racism and supremacy. This makes it all the more vital that those who participate can articulate the difference and necessity of an antiracist white group to the larger community. This is a great topic for the first meeting, so that the group defines their purpose and objectives and will be able to discuss the work skillfully with those who do not attend. You also need to have conversations with the People of Color on your campus before starting the group so they know what the plan is and can, if they choose, serve as accountability partners.

There is also a common misconception that white antiracist groups are a form of navel gazing—the excessive and indulgent self-focus on us at the expense of seeing the bigger picture. Yes, this can be a pitfall, but another move white folks make to avoid looking at their own behavior is saying, "All we are doing is talking about ourselves. When are we actually going to do some work and help our students?" It is uncomfortable to have to look at things we are not proud of or at actions we have done that are inconsistent with how we want to behave and how we want to think of ourselves. Certainly, the primary goal of engaging in antiracist work is to stop the harm to People of Color. But if we defensively jump to fix the system before we see our role in it, we may just replicate the same madness.

Ultimately, our self-reflection informs more strategic action so that we are minimizing harm not only to others, but also to ourselves. This personal work can restore some of what we trade on as white people for the privileges white supremacy offers. When we can only see a Black person as a "threat," a white neighborhood as "good," or children in cages at the border as a "necessary evil," we are broken. Wendell Berry (1970) describes it in another way in his essay "The Hidden Wound":

> *If I had thought it was only black [sic] people who have suffered from the years of slavery and racism, then I could have dealt fully with the matter long ago; I could have filled myself with pity for them, and would no doubt have enjoyed it a great deal and thought highly of myself. But I am sure it's not as simple as that. If white people have suffered less obviously from racism than black people, they have nevertheless suffered greatly; the cost has been greater perhaps than we can yet know. If the white man has inflicted the wound of racism upon black [sic] men, the cost has been that he would receive the mirror image of that wound into himself. As the master, or as a member of the dominant race, he has felt little compunction to acknowledge it or speak of it; the more painful it has grown, the more deeply he has hidden it from himself.* (p. 6)

Without seeing the ways white supremacy clouds our vision, we see only a blurry and distorted world. Intentionally interrogating our own racial conditioning means we no longer avoid looking at the parts we don't want to see. If we wipe away the fog, we can reclaim parts of our humanity.

FOCUS QUESTIONS: UNDERSTANDING OUR RACIAL HISTORY AND ATTITUDES

Do you know the history of how and when your family came to this country? How might whiteness have shaped that experience? Was your family considered white when they first arrived? Or did your family become white over subsequent generations? For example, when my (Elizabeth's) grandparents came to the United States from Italy, they were not considered white. Neither was my father when he went to kindergarten; but when I entered school, I was considered white.

- What family or cultural practice may have been lost in the process of becoming white?
- Did becoming "American" mean your family had to hide or sacrifice part of their identity to gain admittance or acceptance?
- If your family has always been considered white, how has that impacted the way you move through the world?

Common Pitfalls to Avoid

It is important that affinity group meetings have a structure and a sequence. White culture is a strong force, and without guidelines, purpose, and skilled facilitation, affinity meetings can quickly devolve into a breeding ground for more racism.

Colluding. While these groups should be a place where people can make mistakes and practice vulnerability, they also need to be a place where white people hold other white people accountable. And we can both demonstrate care and confront problematic language or behavior. For example, if someone describes a mistake they made, instead of saying, "Oh, I am sure you did not mean it that way!" we say, "Ouch. That sounds hard. Let's talk this through and see what you could have done differently."

Over-intellectualizing. When our understanding of racism comes from an academic place only, we can emphasize our reason and logic to avoid our anxiousness or discomfort. There can be a tendency to live in our heads and not recognize, or to actively avoid, the emotional experience of racism that comes with difficult feelings. Intellect is important, but it is also critical to connect to the emotions that come up around issues of race and racism.

Wanting to "get it right." Perfectionism is the enemy of progress. So, whether it means saying something in spite of the fear of getting it wrong or trying something new even though success is uncertain, we need to make mistakes in order to learn; and there will never be one right answer for ending racism.

Either/or thinking. Either/or thinking is the greatest vehicle for over-simplifying the complexity of racism. People are not either good or bad, and most issues are not simply one thing or another. Be on the lookout for the ways we fall back into a binary mindset to understand human behavior because that will get in the way of the nuanced thinking and creativity that are necessary for dismantling racism.

White silence. Even in antiracism trainings and meetings, participants say things that are based on stereotypes or that are prejudiced, and no one calls it into question. Often, under the guise of kindness and not wanting to embarrass, we have seen even blatantly racist sentiments go unchecked in white antiracist spaces. Perhaps the biggest contribution white people can make in this movement is to ensure racism from other white people never goes uninterrupted. And instead of talking about it *after* the meeting, we say it in the moment. If we cannot at least practice this in a space that is designed to cultivate antiracism, it is unlikely that we will be able to effect change at all.

Wanting to fix other people instead of ourselves. Self-reflection can be uncomfortable. It is far more satisfying to solve other people's problems. When we fixate on other white people's issues, it is usually because they seem familiar (though we may not recognize it) or because we can clearly see them in ourselves. And when our motivation to be antiracist rests on wanting to help only People of Color, our resolve is too easily undone in the face of obstacles. Many times, teachers doing this work shift their attention to how this applies in the classroom or to their specific students. While that is important thinking that ultimately needs to happen, it will not happen with clarity until we first understand ourselves and see how we are participating in the system.

Competition. A common dynamic within white, antiracist spaces is competition. This can manifest in several ways, but usually amounts to trying to be the "wokest" white person, and often includes shaming other white people or making sure others know how just far along they are on their racial journey. "Pushing back," "playing devil's advocate," and questioning someone's use of a term are common forms of this behavior.

Straying away from talking about race. Intersectionality is important, *and* many white people find it easiest to talk about aspects of identity *other* than race, such as social class or gender identity: "I really think what we should be focusing on is social class; that's the real issue." We cannot understand how race impacts our understanding of these other aspects of our identity until we fully understand how race has shaped us. Making sure the group stays focused on race is essential.

Defining the purpose of the group and creating discussion guidelines that help avoid the above pitfalls are vitally important. These will provide a framework for the conversations and a reference point to steer back to when things stray off course. It's also important to share these pitfalls in advance so participants can be on the lookout for them and talk about how to address them when, not if, they arise.

How Do We Know It's Working?

As a result of their participation in antiracist white affinity work, participants develop greater skills and racial literacy, which lead to effective action. Most importantly, participants are able to respond more consistently to racial bias in the moment. They also develop a greater ability to notice their own biased thinking and actions and to engage in conversations that are explicitly about race with other white people and with People of Color. We surveyed people before and after their participation in a facilitated affinity group and found that the vast majority felt they had made progress in all these areas. Additionally, we started to see themes emerge in their comments.

The affinity group was often described as a place to practice systems thinking:

- "I have been noticing how whiteness shows up in me and then places I am in, such as meetings and work."
- "I have greater self-awareness in observing my bias in curriculum and at school in general."

- "I am better at noticing how much I unwittingly participate in white supremacy."

We also found that participants described their shift away from perfectionism and competing with other white people:

- "I am better at spotting my own issues and also forgiving while correcting myself."
- "I have been working to address the fear of getting it wrong and being called out."
- "I find myself connecting and building better relationships with white colleagues rather than trying to be the 'best' white antiracist person."

We saw a pattern among participants grappling with their own barriers and cultivating humility:

- "It showed me that I had a belief that I was more advanced than I was."
- "My own ego and image consciousness have been the biggest barrier for me! I've had a hard time being truly vulnerable and humble because I'm so preoccupied with how I look to others."
- "I seem to think I can outsmart some of the traps that I am not outsmarting. I still catch myself thinking thoughts like, 'I'm not sure I'm strong enough to keep thinking about this right now.'"
- "I realize there is a huge difference between signaling that I am a safe white person and actually being a safe white person."

Participants expressed greater clarity about the ways we as individuals uphold racism and collude with whiteness:

- "I am much more aware of my own whiteness and the constant centering of me and whiteness."
- "Ensuring that white antiracist spaces are not just window dressing. I am thinking about how to partner effectively with People of Color to create change and not take over. Not being passive or

silent, and finding the sweet spot where I'm using my white privilege to advance the cause of racial justice and equity while also centering People of Color."

- "I am working to deepen my empathy while sustaining my anger at oppressive systems so that I don't slip back into the seductiveness of whiteness."

Student Affinity Groups

Once adults on campus understand the how and why of racial affinity spaces and have experienced them firsthand, students can also benefit from the same process. While we recommend that participation in racial affinity groups be optional for students, all adults need to participate in affinity groups as professional development at least *twice* before starting groups for students. Why twice? Because the first time white people sit in an intentional antiracist white affinity space, they are *stressed*. Many are very uncomfortable, and it is during the second session that they settle in and begin to really reflect on their racial identity and what it means. Then, after they have had this experience, we encourage ongoing participation—but it's not mandatory. Again, we see affinity spaces as a way to enhance cross-racial dialogue, not take the place of it. But they are not for everyone, and that's okay, as long as the adults understand the pedagogy. Too often we have seen well-intentioned adults undermine a student affinity space because they didn't understand it or it made them uncomfortable. We also create a place for the facilitators of student affinity groups to meet regularly and reflect on how the groups are progressing, and the configuration of those facilitator groups can be cross-racial or in racial affinity, depending on your programming.

You might be thinking, if the affinity space is optional, what happens with the students who don't opt in? Affinity spaces are one way to think about our racial identity and how it impacts the way we move through school. Another way is to offer cross-racial dialogues at the same time that will also focus on race but not affinity. Sometimes these groups are referred to as a "common ground," "let's talk about race," or "current events" space. Whatever you call it, it's important that this kind of dialogue circle exists alongside the affinity groups. There will always be students and families who will be uncomfortable with affinity groups, so it's helpful to anticipate their concerns. Many years ago when we started a sixth-grade racial affinity groups program, we had about eight white families who did not want their students to participate for many of the reasons we shared earlier in the chapter. Mainly, they assumed that it would be a place of blame and shame and that we were going to make their kids feel bad about being white. So, we sat with those kids during the first meeting to talk about why they didn't feel comfortable joining the white antiracist affinity space. They had a range of responses:

> "My best friend is Black, so I want to be with him."

> "I want to hear what the Kids of Color have to say."

> "I'm not white; I'm Jewish. I've been discriminated against too."

> "I don't see color."

> "It doesn't feel right to split us up by race. Isn't that what segregation was?"

These responses were really helpful because they told us where these kids were in their racial identity development. We could meet them where they were and move forward. They had very good questions and needed a space where they could talk through the tension they felt. What's interesting is that after the first meeting, they all decided to join the white affinity space.

We advocate for racial affinity spaces at the elementary, middle, high, and postsecondary school levels. Like any other aspect of identity, how we understand our race develops over time and can change based on context. Thus, children may have different experiences during particular stages of their development. For example, younger children often don't know why there are different skin colors. So they may need conversations about melanin and geography that affirm the different racial appearances as positive, confirming that differences do not indicate a deficit. Middle schoolers can be very aware of racial groupings, and they are often "trying on" various aspects of popular culture. So they need conversations about how race and racism show up in the media and the images they consume. This is typically the age when white kids start to tell racial jokes, so they are exploring humor and irony when it comes to race. High school students are very aware of how their race plays out both on and off campus, and as they interact with each other and the wider world, they need a place to make sense of their experiences. This is especially important as they distinguish between cultural appreciation and cultural appropriation. They also need to be taught how to interrupt racial bias when they see it because they are noticing how racism is operating as a system. They also usually have more historical information that they are trying to reconcile with current events. Postsecondary groups offer a space not only for ongoing identity development, but also for advocacy and racial justice pursuits that may lead to an area for further study or a career. So, affinity spaces, at each division/level, help students to make sense of themselves and the world and to not become paralyzed in the face of racism.

CURRICULUM EXAMPLE: "POPPING STEREOTYPES" EXERCISE

Fourth graders are very aware of stereotypes, but they often don't have the language to describe what they are seeing, hearing, and feeling. So, we begin by defining the term "stereotype" as a generalization (often an overgeneralization) that is applied to a group of people and is usually based on limited or no background information/knowledge. Stereotypes usually refer to an observed trait or perceived characteristic of the group. We start with age, asking, "Are there stereotypes about kids your age?" In every case, there is then a resounding "Yes!" from the group.

"People think little kids can't do anything."
"They pat us on the head like we're a dog or something, like we're cute but not smart."

"They don't tell us things because they think we can't handle it."

"Adults take over because they think we can't get something done on our own."

Referring back to our identity webs we created at the beginning of the year, we ask each student to generate any stereotypes they have heard about the groups they listed on their web. It's critical that students only generate stereotypes for groups to which *they belong* (you don't want them generating stereotypes about others). Students may comment about their gender identity, "All boys are messy," or their ability, "Kids with dyslexia can't read." For race, we have had white students who wrote, "All white people are rich," and African American students who wrote, "Black neighborhoods are dangerous." Students then partner to work with someone on "popping a stereotype" that they have heard about their group. We use this as an opportunity to teach about ethnographic research, asking them all to become ethnographers for a month. Over the course of four weeks, they will observe and ask questions of their classmates. The goal is to see if they can find at least five examples at school that disprove their stereotype. They are expected to write down their findings. We post all the stereotypes on the wall with an inflated balloon next to the statement. Once the group collects their five examples of behaviors or statements they heard that disprove the stereotype, they can pop their balloon. We love to see students come running in from lunch saying, "We noticed that a table where all boys were sitting was really clean after lunch, but a girls' table was so messy" or, "My friend was telling a story about his block party and how cool it was, and he has mostly Black neighbors. So that breaks the stereotype."

This discussion leads to a conversation about the concept "stereotype threat"—what it is, what it can do to students, and how they can work to interrupt and minimize the effects of stereotypes. It becomes the foundation for our conversations about different forms of discrimination.

To develop our curriculum, we follow the work of Louise Derman-Sparks and her four goals for antibias education (ABE) described in *Anti-Bias Education for Young Children and Ourselves*:

> *Goal 1:* Each child will demonstrate self-awareness, confidence, family pride, and positive social identities.

> *Goal 2:* Each child will express comfort and joy with human diversity, accurate language for human differences, and deep, caring human connections.

> *Goal 3:* Each child will increasingly recognize unfairness, have language to describe unfairness, and understand that unfairness hurts.

> *Goal 4:* Each child will demonstrate empowerment and the skills to act, with others or alone, against prejudice and/or discriminatory actions.

Following these goals, we make sure that white students understand their own identity so they can begin to understand how race shapes their lives and plays out in the culture. Then they need to have accurate language to describe others. Once they have a strong sense of racial difference, they can then engage in productive cross-racial dialogue. They can understand what happened when some people decided to see that difference as a deficit and use it as a weapon to oppress others. If we start with oppression, the lesson can lead to guilt and shame for white children whose only connection to their race is perpetuating racism.

Each time we meet, we inquire, "Are we getting better at understanding what it means to be white?" Many of my students say they are still not sure, but they are seeing things they never saw before. Recently, one white girl ran into our meeting space, anxious to share with me that she had just seen the movie *Black Panther*: "And did you know that almost every person in the movie had brown skin? I've never seen a movie with so many brown people. It was awesome!" We consider it a privilege to be on this racial identity journey with these kids. We often think about what it might have meant for us if we could have had these conversations at their age. And we know that if we can get these kids to understand that racial differences are simply that—just differences—they will not attach notions of deficit to those differences.

We also do an activity called "What's Your Role?" to help students think about how they want to respond when they notice racial stereotype, prejudice, and/or racist belief, language, or action. Given a particular scenario that describes a conflict, students explore each of these roles:

1. Ouch-Feeler
2. Mistake-Maker
3. Bystander
4. Advocate/Ally

First, they brainstorm a time when they felt uncomfortable or noticed something that was happening that they thought was about race. After generating their memories, we discuss the various examples. We then pick a few to role-play. Students work in groups of four and take turns practicing each role. Then we help them reflect on what they learned. Do they have a plan? Do they know what they want to say or do in a particular situation if it happens to them? A typical topic is who's playing with whom on the playground. They describe lots of incidences of white kids not wanting to play with Students of Color, and they often think it's because of race—sometimes it's explicit, sometimes it feels more implicit. We talk about how to navigate those situations and clarify what's going on so everyone can enjoy recess.

Once students finish the year, we survey them about what they learned from the group. We asked our white students to finish the sentence: "Being white at my school means. . ." Here are some of their answers:

- There is a "cloud" around us or a stereotype that all white people are "racist."
- Skin color is not important, but how you are *treated* because of your skin color is important because it [skin color] doesn't change.

- Safer.
- More comfortable talking about race; I don't avoid conversations.
- Feels "normal."
- You should treat others the way you want to be treated.
- What affects us also affects Students of Color.
- That I may not know how Students of Color feel.
- I have the opportunity to learn about how Students of Color feel when they are marginalized and how to speak up when things feel unfair to me based on their example.
- I have to know both mine and the experiences of Students of Color.
- We are in the majority, like a big bag of white rice. And there are a few brown grains of rice mixed in, but they may get pushed to the bottom because there are so many white grains—like we may be pushing them down because there are so many of us.

As we reflect on all we are trying to do in schools, it amazes us that this program takes only about an hour and a half per month. Ninety minutes a month to give these children an opportunity to think deeply about who they are and what that means. When all is said and done, it has been relatively easy to set up this program because there was a will to do it—a clear mandate from school leadership that these conversations matter. It's also important to note that as these fourth graders move through the school, their teachers are commenting on how the students seem different: They are more willing to engage in dialogue around race. And the fifth grade teachers have expanded their curriculum based on the work the students did in fourth grade. The teachers have developed more robust identity units and more explicit ways of examining race and racism. We call that a win–win.

Middle/High School Programming

As noted earlier, older kids benefit from racial affinity group programming that meets them where they are in their identity development. For these groups, we also follow the four goals of antibias education: identity, difference, unfairness, and action. As we design various activities and programming, we make sure we are reaching all four goals and that we are building on each goal and not moving on until we are sure students have demonstrated skill development in a particular area. For example, we try to make sure that students really understand how racism operates as a system (see Curriculum Box in Chapter 5) before we start talking about ways they can interrupt or challenge racism. We also use the following guidelines to ensure that the groups stay focused and have built accountability measures into the program.

Guidelines for White Antiracist Affinity Groups:

1. Affinity groups are hopefully facilitated by at least two or more adults (or older students with younger students) who can address different experiences of white identity, such as intersections of gender identity, social class, religion, etc. Ideally, these facilitators have been trained in affinity group dialogue.
2. Facilitators agree on consistent language/terms that promote greater understanding and clarity for the group's work. This prevents arguments about terms, which would keep participants from fighting the system of racism.
3. The group creates a rationale/statement of philosophy that can be shared with the community, especially at the start of a new school year. It must clearly define what is meant by "antiracist white affinity space" and what the participants hope to develop from their time together.
4. The group needs a curriculum, some kind of "syllabus," that includes activities as well as discussions and that helps frame the discussions.
5. Affinity groups for people who represent a privileged identity examine how that group benefits from, and is supported by, systems of oppression based on the power dynamics in school/society. These privileged affinity groups must not equate their experiences (e.g., shame, guilt, hurt, feeling inadequate) with the oppression experienced by Students of Color. They must investigate the ways their group is often seen as "normal" and/or monolithic. They must also reflect on unequal power distribution, how unearned (as opposed to earned) privilege works (see Curriculum Example in Chapter 5), and the opportunity to serve as an upstander.

6. The group periodically shares highlights with the larger community. This can be done in a way that both preserves the confidentiality of individual group member responses and reflects the larger themes discussed and lessons learned.

7. The group is committed to their own growth and development as well as to development/training of the larger community.

For older students, it's often helpful to think about something they can do with their new knowledge and understanding. For example, one of our high school groups decided to host a white privilege conference for other area high school students and their parents/caregivers. They gathered on a Saturday and held different workshops for both students and adults (see Appendix A for a description of their opening activity). It was so powerful to see a room full of white young adults engaged in important, reflective conversations about their race and their participation in racism.

How ever you decide to pursue greater racial literacy, there is great value in having white teachers and students working together to uncover, illuminate, and practice ways of interrupting white supremacy. By developing a group identity committed to antiracism, we can move away from our individual concepts of racism and see how we are all part of a larger system. And in antiracist white affinity spaces, we can improve our skills without causing more harm to People of Color. Together, we have an opportunity to dismantle racism that is not possible in isolation.

ACTIVITY: CASE STUDIES FOR STUDENTS

Please read these scenarios as a group and consider the following questions:

- What are the core issues or problems presented? What's really going on? How do we know?
- What are the various perspectives? How is "difference" operating?

- Are there stereotypes present? What are the power dynamics?
- What actions would you suggest?

1. At the middle school's annual Halloween assembly, which is really a "best costume" contest, you, the student body president, are the emcee organizing students to walk before the judges. As the contestants are lining up on stage, you see someone wearing a police uniform with the words "Border Patrol" on the back. He's walking next to another student dressed up in a poncho and big Mexican-style hat, including a fake moustache. They are laughing, and the "Mexican" keeps running away as the "agent" tries to catch him. What should you do?

2. Seniors are starting to hear about college acceptances. You are sitting out in the hallway doing some work when two white students walk by. One is in tears because she just heard that she didn't get into her favorite school. Her friend is consoling her, and you hear that they are even more upset that an African American student from their class got in. You hear one of the students say, "She only got in because she's Black." You know both students. Should you get involved? If so, how?

CHAPTER 5

Rooting and Shifting: Rethinking Pedagogical Approaches and Curricular Topics

Just as schools were once rushing to adopt antibullying curricula, they are currently grappling with the idea of a formal curriculum to explicitly teach about bias and racism. This is an important shift, as many teachers avoid teaching or talking about race all together. They worry that it may expose their political leanings and influence impressionable children. They're also concerned that parents may accuse them of indoctrinating their children with a particular agenda. Though the absence of talking explicitly about race is often regarded as neutral, it is anything but. That silence keeps the status quo firmly in place. So, to not talk about race is just as political as talking about it.

The irony is that in a recent survey by the nonpartisan group America's Promise Alliance, 56% of students reported that they had the opportunity to discuss racism "sometimes or a great deal," but that those experiences varied widely. And they found that most students were *not* having substantive conversations about race in their school. So, many of the reports of an overwhelming number of "divisive" curricular topics are, at best, overstated. Yet, the benefits of having conversations about race and racism have been consistently reported. The same survey also states that conversations about race and racism set students up for success after graduation and make them more apt to speak up against injustice. Additionally, numerous studies have shown that students are *more* engaged in school after taking classes that address race and racism directly (Barnum, 2021).

Some states have passed legislation requiring schools to highlight implicit bias, diversity, equity, inclusion, and belonging in connection to race and ethnicity. At the same time, other states are passing, or attempting to pass, legislation that restricts how teachers can talk about racism or sexism, primarily by banning particular words. Most of these latter bills mimic phrasing from the 1776 Commission Report, released by the Trump administration, seeking to ensure that no one feels guilt, discomfort, or any other "form of psychological distress because of their race or sex." In either case, these mandates will mostly be left to individual schools and educators to interpret and decide how to implement these initiatives.

We have outlined how understanding our own racial identity is foundational for change, and the same is true for our students. Curricula can be an arena for creating opportunities for students to get grounded in their own identity, to consider differences, and to take action against injustices. In this chapter we will look at pedagogical approaches to developing racial literacy and offer some curricular resources, as examples of what teaching about race and racism might look like, and some strategies for confronting resistance and building momentum for change.

For years, discussions that were explicitly about identity in general and race specifically were typically reserved for advisory/homeroom, social emotional learning, or health curricula. The idea of building empathy as the key to undoing prejudice and bullying has been a popular strategy within education for decades. The philosophy of walking in someone else's shoes has given way to hours of lessons, including some disastrous simulations and role-playing activities. We have seen photos of teachers standing over students and acting as slave owners while other students lie in cramped spaces, ostensibly experiencing what it would have felt like to be a slave during the Middle Passage. We have also heard of cotton-picking simulations, in which a group of young children were sent out on a field of artificial turf with bags slung over their shoulders and told to pick up cotton balls that were strewn across the field. Not only can these activities be horrifying for the students who are having a part of their traumatic history minimized and simplified into an hour-long lesson, but many white students feel as though they are playing a game and then go back to life as usual.

We are skeptical that any long-term change arises from these activities because there is little evidence that empathy-building has prevented either adults or students from acting on implicit bias and fear of racial differences. These activities ignore and erase how racism operates as a system, into which we are all carefully socialized. We see oppression and exception tropes when we ask teachers to do a curriculum audit by race. They enumerate each instance where students will see their racial identity reflected in the curriculum. Too often, race is only explicitly named and studied through racial atrocities. For instance, African American identity is only mentioned in a unit on enslavement or civil rights; Asian American identity is only named when examining Japanese incarceration during World War II; Latinx identity emerges only in the struggle for farmworkers' rights; Native identity ends in the 19th century in a diorama of "how they lived" before they all went away. And white people are only raced when they are identified as oppressors, creating feelings of guilt and shame. The other way race shows up is when Individuals of Color overcome their circumstances, despite the odds. These lessons feed the narrative that "anyone can make it if they try hard enough," which leads to the belief that anyone who fails must be deficient. Again, this takes the emphasis off being able to see systems and lays the responsibility at the feet of individuals.

Though it is absolutely necessary to help children understand how racial oppression operates, white children need to know they have a racial identity *before* we teach them about systemic racism. While interviewing middle school students, one white boy commented on how he assumed the purpose of their study of slavery was to make all the white kids "feel bad, like some kind of punishment." Too often, white children do not learn about their whiteness because, as the dominant culture, it goes unnamed and unmarked. So, race is reduced to something that Children of Color have and racism is something that "bad" white people do to People of Color. Thus, we have positioned these children as antagonists in matters of race instead of helping them understand how they can work together with People of Color to defeat racism.

CURRICULUM EXAMPLE:
WHITE ANTIRACIST ACTIVISM

To help all students to have a greater sense of multiracial solidarity, we encourage the exploration of both People of Color and white people who have stood up in the face of racism. In particular, we offer the model of white antiracism because white children are often unaware of people who look like them and have fought for racial justice. It's critical that these students be given the opportunity to identify with and learn from these activists so that they can develop their own skills and be a force for positive change.

In studying and learning from these activists, we offer these critical questions for consideration:

1. Consider the activists' lives. What were the significant moments that led to their activism? What motivated them to work for change?
2. What skills do/did they need to challenge racial injustice?
3. What unconscious or hidden bias/perspectives might these activists have?
4. How can white people work effectively in solidarity with People of Color?
5. How do the activists keep from replicating the very system they are trying to challenge?
6. What is the value of a multiracial, antiracist coalition?
7. What actions might you take to work for racial justice?

See Appendix B for a fuller description and suggested list of white antiracist activists you could explore with your class.

One of the best related metaphors we have found is the concept of "rooting and shifting" (Yuval-Davis, 1997). Developed by a group of Italian feminists, the concept makes clear that we enter effective dialogue with others only by being rooted in our own identity. Being grounded in who we are enables us to shift to understand the experiences of those who are different from us. In other words, this dialogic exchange requires that we have a strong understanding of who we are before we can effectively engage with people who have different perspectives and different lived experiences. When applied to racial identity, this means we first need to know our own racial history, identity, and lived experience before we can effectively engage with others about theirs. And this affirmation of difference can help prevent feelings of superiority or inferiority and can allow students to grasp a greater racial complexity that does not incite the need for categorizing some as "better" and others as "less than." It is not an either/or world, so we need to stop offering students simplistic and inaccurate versions of history and race. We need teachers to develop more critical and accurate narratives, nuanced portraits that embrace racial identity *and* challenge racism.

There is much to be learned from parents of Students of Color who affirm and root their children in their culture so that they will be less impacted by messages of inferiority. These children are better able to resist racist messages that come at them (Stevenson, 2014). We can do something similar for white kids so that they stop getting stuck in shame *and* they are less likely to internalize superiority. Students who are confident in who they are are better equipped to grapple with systemic oppression and not feel like it is a personal attack. So, when thinking about curriculum development, teachers need to begin by affirming the racial identity of each student. Only then are students in a position to share their identity with others, learn from their peers, and engage in the study of racism in our nation's founding, history, and current culture.

CURRICULUM EXAMPLE: DR. MARTIN LUTHER KING JR. DAY CELEBRATIONS

In classrooms around the country, we know that many elementary teachers are finishing their Martin Luther King Jr. unit during the month of January, perhaps even having an assembly held around Martin Luther King Jr. Day. While it is crucial that all children know about Dr. King and what he stood for, one of the main takeaways for white children is often that Dr. King was killed by a racist white man. In other words, they may come away from the lesson believing that white equals racist. They can also come away thinking only character matters, leading to more color-evasiveness. This kind of piecemeal racial education is what drives some older white children to roll their eyes when we say we are going to have a conversation about race. We have set them up for confusion and shame. They ask, "Why do I want to talk about something that just says how bad I am?" We must teach about injustice, but we need to offer a different way forward for white students. We need to teach them that as soon as oppression begins, resistance forms to challenge inequity. People of Color have had agency and have always been change makers, and many white people have also stood in solidarity with those who fought racism. We have to tell those stories so white children have antiracist role models who look like them. During our fourth- and fifth-grade white affinity group conversations, we read *She Stood for Freedom*, a book about Joan Mulholland, a white civil rights activist and Freedom Rider. The students have so many questions, and the vast majority say that this is the first time they have ever learned about a white person who was fighting racism. The goal is to help students understand that the study of Dr. King is critical to their learning and is enhanced when paired with cross-racial examples of solidarity and accountability. (See also Appendix B, White Antiracist Activists.)

Once students are firmly rooted in the complexity of their racial identity, how can we make the naming of, noticing of, and discussion of racial difference the rule and not the exception? How can we look critically at the racial implications of curricula and name whiteness so that it removes it as the default baseline? How can these steps lead to important conversations with our students about racial differences and power imbalances?

Many of the schools we work with prioritize changing the curriculum to reflect a more racially diverse world as a way to move toward racial equity. This work is crucial. All students need to see themselves and their experiences reflected and validated at school. And as we noted in the discussion of the ABE goals in Chapter 4, they also need to develop their consciousness around difference. Curriculum changes are concrete, but without a simultaneous effort by teachers to be racially literate and to examine their pedagogy, the good intentions behind diversifying the curriculum can still cause harm. Some schools may even make radical shifts in the materials they teach but continue to avoid the discussion of race and racism all together. As one curriculum supervisor told us, she had a teacher teach *The Kite Runner*, but told her students to "skip Chapter 9 because something bad happens."

Many educators can articulate why they should have a more diverse curriculum: "We want kids to connect to the material." "All students should see themselves reflected in what we teach." "We want to prepare our students for a diverse world." All of this is true, and yet, when it comes to taking old classics, topics, and units out of curriculum in favor of including a diversity of perspectives, we have seen, again and again, resistance from white educators. Basically, they want to have their cake and eat it too. They'll make changes, but only the ones that don't force them to give up what they love or what has worked "all these years."

As long as white teachers determine what is an important concept, critical "knowledge," or "good" literature (and therefore worthy of study) without examining how their own experience has informed their opinions, then all of the resources, book lists, and curriculum audits in the world will not change white curricular dominance. Teachers hold sacred the things that they valued in their own education experience, and they often see those as impartial standards: "This is what good writing is." There is no awareness of their own subjectivity nor acknowledgment of how they came to believe that certain things are just "true." And they continue to reinforce patterns of exceptionalism by offering up one text (usually the summer reading assignment) or unit revolving around a Person of Color as evidence of their "embrace of diversity." This logic does not consider the ways exposure to and experiences of linguistic and cultural variety impact our perception of and appreciation for what counts as "good."

Similarly, content is too often scrutinized with the same biased approach. Perhaps if white teachers had firsthand experience of the trauma that the N-word still causes Black people, we would be less able to justify (in the name of "illuminating attitudes" of a particular era) teaching some of the books and curricula that use that word. It's interesting that a teacher will fight to keep *To Kill a Mockingbird* or *The Adventures of Huckleberry Finn* and justify the use of the N-word in those texts as "historically accurate." However, the mention of sexual development or the use of the F-bomb in a book by a Writer of Color often renders a book unteachable. In a recent interview with Trevor Noah (2019), Angie Thomas, author of *The Hate U Give*, said, "There are 89 instances of the F-word in *The Hate U Give*. . . but last year alone, over 800 people lost their lives to police brutality, and that number is far scarier. So when you're telling me it's the language, no, that's not what it is. You don't want to talk about the topic." Which forms of violence are deemed appropriate and essential learning in our classrooms, and who decides?

If we don't question our curricular selections and priorities, we will continue to replicate a world where the white voice, experience, and values are heralded as true knowledge. And students will continue to be inculcated into the philosophy of a limited hierarchy of what is "important." Instead of focusing on a narrow and questionable standard of educational merit, we should be asking ourselves essential questions about what we are trying to achieve in our classes. How can we offer some context to what we teach so that the content resonates more deeply? How can we teach students to recognize and value multiple perspectives and truths and to see the world in a new way and with more texture and nuance?

By making Writers, Thinkers, and Inventors of Color adjunct, by ignoring their many and vast contributions, we also send the message that students are not missing anything by not studying them. This is a problem not just because Students of Color are *not* seeing themselves reflected in the majority of curriculum we teach in schools. It is also a problem because white students see their race and culture *predominantly* represented. What happens when you see yourself reflected at the center of every curriculum over the course of your education? We are signaling to Students of Color that their personal and cultural experiences are less valuable than those of white students. We also reinforce a mentality of cultural superiority by letting our white students believe that white culture is what is worth knowing, and there is no loss in knowing *only* that. We are setting up our white students to continue to be self-referential and unable to look at their world with a truly critical eye.

From her research, Brené Brown (2007) concluded that to feel curiosity about a subject requires knowing, even a little bit, about it. For example, it wasn't until I (Jenna) had learned about romanticism that I was able to fully appreciate Mary Shelley's *Frankenstein*. Once I understood some things about the Harlem Renaissance, I developed a deeper connection to the words and work of Zora Neale Hurston. So why couldn't it be true that, with some curiosity about subjects we do not know much about, what we see as important could shift? It is not simply a matter of discerning what is important within a white-dominated world. Context matters and can also allow people to look into something unfamiliar and see beauty and value where it is often overlooked.

This was the case for me (Elizabeth) when I decided to add Leslie Marmon Silko's novel *Ceremony* to my syllabus. *Ceremony* was the first Native American novel I had ever taught, and I had to do a lot of context-setting with my students because they were so unfamiliar with a text that didn't follow a linear, Eurocentric timeline and format. *Ceremony* tells the story of a Laguna Pueblo war veteran who returns home. Via the structure of the text, Silko unsettles the reader just as the main character is dislocated and struggling to reconnect with his sense of self, family, and ancient traditions of his culture that will restore him and his people. We did background reading on Silko to learn more about her life and context, and we invited a Native scholar to teach us more about many of the traditions, symbols, and themes referred to in the text. The timeline of the novel jumps around, and my students kept getting confused as to what was happening. I finally realized I couldn't teach this book the same way that I approached my other texts, and I just let them read the entire book first—just turning pages, no notes—before we started discussing it. That way they could get the plot down so they knew what was happening and could focus on the details, language, and beautiful nuance of the story. I had never done that before, but because the students had never read a novel written by a Native person, we had to slow down to fill in the gaps in their knowledge. And it really paid off. Most said it was the most challenging but ultimately the most interesting and compelling novel they had ever read. But they really fought me at the beginning because the novel was so different from anything they had ever read in school before. It really highlighted for me what a disservice we do to students when we limit what they read based on what we are familiar with and think is "great" literature.

Naming Whiteness

Early in my middle-school English teaching days, I (Jenna) started to realize that I only talked about the race of an author, or how the author's race and culture impacted the writing, if the author was a Person of Color. So, I started to experiment by announcing white authors as "white" when introducing a new novel to my students and by adding discussion questions about how the author's race might impact the story and writing style. Somehow, I thought this would be a bigger deal than it was. For the most part, my students took it in stride as though it were perfectly normal to name whiteness. Perhaps my delivery of this information was matter of fact, and so it did not seem an oddity. Or maybe the act of taking something implicit and making it explicit is something many of us crave. As Lisa Delpit (1995) explains in *Other People's Children: Cultural Conflict in the Classroom*,

> *We all interpret behaviors, information, and situations through our own cultural lenses; these lenses operate involuntarily, below the level of conscious awareness, making it seem that our own view is simply "the way it is." . . . We must consciously and voluntarily make our cultural lenses apparent.* (p. 151)

When white teachers avoid naming whiteness, when we remain silent about race when race is clearly a factor in the classroom or curriculum, we are in fact teaching ideological and institutional aspects of whiteness. In effect, we are saying that whiteness is the norm (there are "authors" and there are "Authors of Color") and that racism is either imagined or not worth talking about. The silence is a de facto denial of privileges and oppressions. We often hear teachers object: How do we add the objective of naming whiteness to our curriculum when we already feel overloaded with teaching skills and content? It's a question worth addressing. But we also need to be clear: By not making the privileges and assumptions of whiteness explicit, we maintain whiteness as "normal."

Years ago, my (Jenna's) sixth graders read *Brown Girl Dreaming*, by Jacqueline Woodson, for their summer reading. After they discussed the novel for a few days, I asked, "What if this book were called *White Girl Dreaming*? Would it be a different book?" Instantly, an African American boy raised his hand. "It could not be the same book," he said. "When you are Black, forgetting about racism is like trying to forget a song that plays on the radio twenty-four hours a day. Even when you want to forget it, it is still playing."

With this perspective on the table, we started a conversation, gingerly dipping our toes in. The class began to discuss how white people can choose to forget the song—to ignore the impact of race. Although I could feel some kind of energy or excitement, from the Students of Color—that we were actually discussing this—I became worried that I was making my white students feel guilty, so we quickly moved on. I had the power in that room as the teacher, and I shut down the conversation.

I knew, even though perhaps I couldn't have articulated it, that just like my sixth grader who made this heartbreaking radio-song analogy, some of my students were already aware, sometimes painfully aware, of racism and privilege. But I was afraid that I could not control the conversation. I was afraid that someone might say something hurtful. I was worried that in my white ignorance, I could make things worse for my Students of Color in a racially imbalanced classroom.

Without meaning to, I had silenced my students. I had prioritized protecting the white fragility of my white students over encouraging the eagerness of my Students of Color. I wonder now if my white students actually were that fragile or if I shut things down for my own projection of discomfort. How were my own feelings influencing my teaching? In what ways did I stand in the way of healthy identity development and racial literacy for all my students by stopping the conversation? Did my lack of skill cause racial stress for some of my students by my not fully engaging in the conversation? What message did that send to my white students, and what message did it send to my Students of Color? We need to pay attention to the seemingly small moments and reflect on them. We need to unpack the myriad ways our curriculum is already shaped by race—and how we want to respond.

Later, in that same sixth-grade class, we discussed how we knew that the characters in *A Separate Peace*, by John Knowles, were white. That same African American student said, "Because they don't mention it. They don't mention it because they don't have a problem with race. People only know about race if they have had a problem with it." This time, we did wade in. We discussed this in detail. Was segregation in effect during this time period? If so, what was its impact on the characters in this story? How did we know the author was white without a picture of him? What are the effects of white people never naming their race? The conversation was not perfect, but we had it. We, as a class, had built up our race muscles enough over the year to wade into it and not turn back.

That year, I started a new practice. After each class, I would set a timer for three minutes and reflect on these questions. I wrote in bullet points, and if I had no response to a particular question that day, I skipped it.

1. Did I make assumptions about how the kids would respond to the lesson/class, and if so, was I right? Were there any patterns to my assumptions based on race, gender, ability, social class, etc.?
2. How did I feel while teaching this lesson? Were there moments I felt anxious or worried?
3. Did I notice any students seeming anxious around the topic? Were there any patterns to who was vocal in class today?
4. In what ways was I teaching what I know? Is there an additional perspective I could have added for my students' understanding?
5. What could I do differently next time?

I read over these reflections at the end of each week before I prepared for the next week's lessons. Eventually, I got a little more brave and recorded a class on an iPad, so that I could look more intentionally at what I was saying and the responses of my students. Truthfully, these efforts were fairly minimal in terms of time investment and yet, this reflection made a big impact on my teaching. I made small adjustments over time, but I could also see the level of comfort, the climate of taking risks, and the complexity of thinking increase dramatically in what my students wrote and talked about. It reinforced my understanding of how engaging racial diversity in a classroom can increase creativity, improve collaboration, and develop our problem-solving skills (Page, 2008).

CURRICULUM EXAMPLE:
A NOTE ABOUT WHITE PRIVILEGE

Some teachers want to introduce the concept of "white privilege," a term that often causes stress for white students. The term refers to the advantage that white people receive because they are not the targets of racism. Yet, perhaps even more importantly, it also speaks to a *lack of obstacles*—all the things white people *don't* have to deal with because of their race. The term can often make white students defensive, saying things like, "I didn't ask to be born white," or "It's not my fault that I'm white," or "I've worked very hard for everything I've accomplished." Because they don't want to be perceived as racist, they reject any notion of privilege.

To counteract that defensiveness, we find it helpful to distinguish between "earned" and "unearned" privilege. We start with having students think about privileges they earn (e.g., weekly allowance for chores, time playing video games online once their homework is done, babysitting in the neighborhood once they completed a safety course, etc.). Once they can detail their own list, we shift to talk about the things they get without even asking for them. We talk about aspects of identity and how that can affect what they can and cannot do. We first consider age: what do they get to do just because they get older? They talk about being allowed to get their driver's license once they turn 16. We consider their gender identity/expression and how that impacts how they move through the world. Do boys and girls have different considerations? What about transgender students? Or gender nonbinary students? Are their experiences different from cisgender students? Students share their experiences based on their particular identity, and we ask them not to generalize about the experiences of others. They are comparing their various personal positions and experiences.

With this foundation, we move into issues of race and ethnicity. Students discuss recent events and talk about how race can impact the way people see and treat you. We find that this process enables students to move from talking about "earned" privilege to talking about "unearned" privilege without becoming defensive. They see that there is a larger system that impacts the way race is perceived and noticed. Once they are aware of it, they can be more thoughtful and considerate of how they are perceived—and what that means for people who are different.

Identity and Skill Development for Students

As white teachers are interrogating their pedagogical moves and analyzing how their identity shows up in their teaching, they can begin to think about how to develop these same racial literacy skills for their students: do they understand that they have a race and that there are both historical and current social structures that have influenced how their race is perceived and understood? This knowledge becomes a foundation on which to build an understanding of racism and then to develop the skills to dismantle that system of oppression and challenge unearned white-skin privilege.

There are too many variables in terms of context, age/grade level, and subject area to offer a one-size-fits-all plan for every teacher. This work is personal and needs to grow out of your unique experience and environment. However, the questions below provide teachers with markers to assess antiracist skill development. The goal is to have students' work demonstrate understanding in each of these areas:

1. Do my students have a foundational understanding of race, both as a social construct and as a lived reality?
   a. Can they describe their own racial identity? (Skin color/melanin, other aspects of their physiognomy, ancestors, history, culture)
   b. Do they have accurate language to describe the racial identity of others? (Terminology, history, culture, solidarity)
   c. Do they have a sense of their own group membership around race?
   d. Can they see how race goes beyond an individual's skin color to see how society views race?

2. Do my students understand racism as a system?
   a. In the past?
   b. In the present?

3. Do my students know how to identify and name racial injustice? Do they understand unfairness and how it impacts the larger community? Do they have a critical understanding of how racial inequity impacts everyone in significant ways?

4. Can my students identify and name models of resistance to racism?

5. Can my students identify and name models of antiracism within Communities of Color? With white people in solidarity with People of Color?

The curricular examples shared throughout this chapter provide ideas for how you might generate evidence of growth in these various areas. We have also included a list of resources at the end of the chapter.

**CURRICULUM EXAMPLE:
TEACHING THE CYCLE OF OPPRESSION**

A tension we observe frequently in schools is the dialogue around what's "racist." Walking down the hallway of a middle school, we observe students grabbing their backpacks for lunch. A white student says to another white student, "Can you hand me my backpack?" and their friend asks, "Which one?" The white student replies, "The black one," and the comments fly: "That's so racist!" "You can't say that!" Here is a prime example of the noticing of color—even with a common object—as the presence of racism. Students can be quick to throw around the term "racist," but often have no real understanding of its meaning and relationship to stereotypes, prejudice, and discrimination.

We have found it helpful to teach the cycle of oppression (see graphic in Appendix C) by walking through each step of the cycle to clarify terms (e.g., Where does fear of difference come from? What's a stereotype? What is the difference between prejudice and discrimination? What does it mean to have internalized superiority or inferiority?) and to see how they build on each other to create oppressive systems and spaces. (See Curriculum Example on "Popping Stereotypes" in Chapter 4 for another idea about teaching the cycle of oppression.)

Widening the Analysis

Having discussions within collegial teams ensures that white people can be more aware of what they don't know so they are not making decisions in isolation. Exploring the development of antiracist skills as a team also enables students to have a more consistent experience. On multiracial teams, it is critical that white teachers do not put more burden on Teachers of Color and expect them to solve all issues related to race. If a team is primarily or all white teachers, how might you include more Voices of Color? How can you engage parents and/or other members of the community to broaden your reflection? Inspired by Zaretta

Hammond's (2014) work on culture in her book, *Culturally Responsive Teaching and the Brain,* here are some questions that can help illuminate and clarify any underlying assumptions that may be operating and embedded in the current curriculum. They can also help identify possible areas for shifts as well as opportunities for more skill development.

1. What are the unconscious beliefs, norms, and values of your team or department?
2. What are the unspoken rules and hidden curricula of your team or department?
3. How would you describe the ideal student for your curriculum? What assumptions do you have about their background, culture, and language?
4. What messages do you believe students receive about race via your grade level/department's curricula?
5. Are there any assumptions/biases built into your criteria for your assessments/evaluations? Do they create an advantage for certain students?

One middle school math team who worked through these questions was able to bring to light the ways that whiteness was the unspoken center of their seemingly objective curricula. In an attempt to improve the performance of historically underrepresented students in math and to narrow the "achievement gap," the department had previously put all their effort on bolstering individual students by focusing solely on remediation practices. Realizing this was not effective, the department changed their focus to reevaluating their curriculum: instead of trying to fix kids, they wanted to fix the system.

The department embedded opportunities to intentionally expose all students to Mathematicians of Color. They made explicit that many math concepts are wrongfully attributed to white mathematicians instead of Mathematicians of Color. They sought to increase and validate multiple strategies for problem solving. They evaluated lessons to ensure that the value of math was not only described in the abstract, but also useful in everyday life. They recognized their pedagogy had only valued individual achievement, and they created more opportunities for students to collaborate, work in groups, and teach each other. They made explicit some of the ways mathematics had been used as a tool to uphold and support racist beliefs.

This math department changed their curriculum significantly, and they saw an equally dramatic shift in the level of engagement in all their students. They stopped talking about student "achievement gaps" and instead focused on their teacher "expectation gaps," the ways teachers expected less of certain students based on implicit bias and stereotypes. Thus, by taking a collaborative and team-based approach to their problem, they saw how it was their design and content that was getting in the way of all children experiencing success in their classes.

By including other members of grade-level teams, departments, and/or divisions, we can start to shift the whole culture rather than creating siloed pockets where equity work is happening. Therefore, our work together is an important step to extending our learning about ourselves beyond our individual classroom walls. We are always better together.

CURRICULUM EXAMPLE: NUMBERS DON'T LIE— WHO CONTROLS THE INFORMATION?

(Inspired by participants at the Multicultural Teaching Institute)

Tenth-grade students are given several graphs, from newspapers, magazines, journals, and textbooks, that show a variety of ways of displaying numerical data. They are asked to identify the main point of each graph and answer four questions: What was the creator's purpose? Is there an obvious bias? Were units chosen to skew the data? Do the numbers lie? Students are also asked to report the basics of each graph: descriptive title, labeled axes, range of values, and appropriate units.

In pairs, students research one of the topics to find data representing multiple perspectives on the issue. Topics include drug use versus incarceration along racial lines; gun ownership, rural versus urban; females in leadership roles in Fortune 500 companies versus MBA degrees granted to women; profiling in traffic stops/arrests; immigrants and crime data; employment rates versus government assistance use.

As students research their topic, they graph the data and prepare to explain why they chose to create the graph they did and how they chose the scale they used. As a team, they prepare a presentation about how data can be used to make different arguments based on one's perspective/experience.

After reporting their findings, students journal about what they would want to study next and the main lessons of what they learned about the media's presentation of data. They reflect on the following questions: Does one graph tell an entire story? Who is telling the story behind each graph? Whose perspective is not represented? Why might that be? How could these graphs be used to reinforce stereotypes? How could injustices be supported by generalizations that are found in the data?

Curriculum Resources to Support Making Change

There are many amazing resources that outline questions and procedures for analyzing current curricula and for potential additions for racial equity. We also encourage looking beyond traditional mediums and finding ways to bring in forms of media that students are familiar with and find engaging, such as blogs, podcasts, and videos. Here are some of the resources we utilize frequently. Our appreciation to all these authors, scholars, and teachers.

Texts

Culturally Responsive Teaching and Brain: Promoting Authentic Engagement and Rigor Among Culturally and Linguistically Diverse Students by Zaretta Hammond

Cultivating Genius: An Equity Framework for Culturally and Historically Responsive Literacy by Gholdy Muhammad

Anti-Bias Education for Young Children and Ourselves (2nd ed.) by Louise Derman-Sparks, Julie Olsen Edwards, and Catherine M. Goins

Websites & Social Media

American Indians In Children's Literature:
americanindiansinchildrensliterature.blogspot.com

#disrupttexts (Twitter)

Learning for Justice:
learningforjustice.org

Southern Poverty Law Center—Teaching Hard History:
https://www.splcenter.org/20180131/teaching-hard-history

Rethinking Schools:
rethinkingschools.org

Teaching for Change:
teachingforchange.org

Social Justice Books:
socialjusticebooks.org

Project 1619:
https://www.nytimes.com/interactive/2019/08/14/magazine/1619
-america-slavery.html

Facing History and Ourselves:
facinghistory.org

Specific to Math/Science

The Algebra Project:
algebra.org/wp/

Radical Math:
radicalmath.org

Equitable Math:
equitablemath.org

The Underrepresentation Curriculum Project:
underrep.com

We also have a number of resources available on our website, Teaching While White, www.teachingwhilewhite.org.

CASE STUDY: TO TEACH OR TO KILL A MOCKINGBIRD

The highlight of this white teacher's eighth grade spring term is the unit she teaches on Harper Lee's *To Kill a Mockingbird*. She has taught the novel for years, and the feedback from students during discussions is always so positive. She read the book when she was in eighth grade, and it's the one she best remembers from her school days—so teaching it feels right. But during a recent lunch conversation, a Colleague of Color asked her why she still teaches the book. The white teacher gave her a list of reasons: the beautiful narrative, the theme of challenging racism during the civil rights period, the point of view of the narrator as a child their age, etc. Then her colleague asked a follow-up question that really made her stop and think: "Who do you think that book was written for?" Her colleague told her how much she hated reading that book when she was in eighth grade, and then she excused herself to get back to class. The white teacher started to wonder if her impressions of the book were based on her reading it as a white girl. Given that the novel portrays both white and Black characters, she never really thought that students may experience the text differently based on their race. She really felt the temperature in the room go up while having the conversation with her colleague. In fact, she felt kind of nervous about continuing the dialogue and was secretly relieved when her colleague got up to leave. What should she do next?

General Discussion Questions:

1. How is whiteness operating in this example?
2. How is racial equity impacted by this scenario?
3. What actions would you suggest?

Case Study Specific Questions:

1. Would the teacher have been as uncomfortable answering the questions about the novel if a white person asked them? Why or why not?
2. How does the teacher know if all the students enjoy the book? How do you gage that in a classroom? How do you know the experience of your students?
3. Is it clear what themes, topics, and skills you want to address by teaching particular texts? Or do you tend to teach what you love? At what cost?
4. Is this the best/only text to teach these objectives?
5. What perspectives are missing within this text?
6. What tropes or stereotypes might it reinforce?
7. Is there a way to teach this text in a way that examines cultural biases and assumptions?

CHAPTER 6

Assessment and Feedback

Once we start making these shifts to curricula, how do teachers know that they are making progress? And how can we measure the effectiveness of the changes we make to both pedagogy and content? At the end of the day, all our work to make our schools effectively antiracist will only happen if we hold ourselves and our systems accountable. To date, most of our racial equity work has happened on a voluntary basis, and even when institutions have completed mandatory training on a particular topic, we rarely see schools adopt assessment protocols that would document the shifts teachers and educators make based on their professional development. In general, our assessment practices for the adults and the institution have been underutilized. That's a big reason why racism remains so firmly entrenched, and it's one of the areas we can make the most significant impact.

One of the most underrated skills for challenging racism is the ability to give and receive effective feedback. Schools are notorious for having either no real system of evaluation or one that is not useful to teachers. And teachers are often reluctant to get feedback from students and to use it in productive ways. We will share examples for evaluating the quality of student–teacher relationships in the classroom. We will also share assessment strategies that can test for and minimize racial bias in grading and student feedback.

ACT Skills Protocol

As a diagnostic tool, we developed our ACT (analyze, communicate, and teach) skills protocol for educators to guide them through issues or conflicts. By answering this series of questions, teachers can efficiently self-assess where they are and what they need to focus on to improve their antiracist practice:

> *Analyze*: Can I see whiteness operating? Do I have self-knowledge of what it means for me to be white? Do I understand the process of white identity development? Can I see how and where whiteness shows up?

> *Communicate*: Can I name whiteness? Describe it? Speak to it? Interrupt it? Redirect?

> *Teach*: Can I enable others to learn how whiteness works? Explain structural racism? Develop curricula? Assess student skills in the areas of racial identity and challenging racism?

Each of these skills can be developed and practiced in different settings. As detailed in Chapter 4, affinity groups are a great place to *analyze* how we have been socialized to be white. This collegial space can provide reflection as well as somewhere to ask questions and learn new information. Some white teachers prefer to read the stories of other white educators. The "Understanding our Racial History and Attitudes" activity in Chapter 4 can also help answer these questions.

This first step of the protocol roots white teachers in their identity so they can look at how their positionality affects their ability to *communicate*, and practice becomes the key to this next skill. First, educators must start identifying themselves as white *out loud*, meaning an observable engagement in conversations about race that include whiteness. They must actively ask how their race is showing up, how it might affect the way they work with colleagues, students, and families. If they feel stressed in a conversation with People of Color, they notice how the stress impacts their ability to listen and intervene, such as by saying, "Wow, I'm really feeling stressed. My stomach is getting tight.

Let me get a glass of water and come right back." Dr. Howard Stevenson describes this as our ability to calculate, locate, and communicate our uncomfortable feelings when navigating cross-racial interactions. When educators hear stereotypes or racially disparaging comments about People of Color, they can then speak up: "That comment makes me really uncomfortable," or "Something about what you said is not sitting right with me." We must improve our ability to engage with other white people and not let these kinds of comments go by unaddressed, not even via our silence.

Finally, educators must bring this work into their classrooms and design curricula that support white students to engage in a similar process. Educators must *teach* about racial identity as detailed in Chapter 5, modeling their identity development for students. By creating space for conversations about race and racism, classrooms can become sites for transformation. To develop effective pedagogical and curricular approaches, teachers need to consider assessment strategies and how race may impact how they design lessons and how they evaluate both students and themselves.

Assessing Our Relationships With Students

One of the biggest barriers we face is that the vast majority of white teachers believe *deeply* that they cannot possibly be racist toward their students. In fact, they condemn racism, and so they believe there is no possibility that what they are doing with children could be racist. They see themselves as nice teachers who love their students. And yet, they have feelings of discomfort and anxiety toward Students of Color that go unacknowledged. They have uninterrogated stereotypes about Students and Families of Color that seep into their classrooms about: who can achieve and who may not be quite up to the task; who works hard and who does not; who engages and who does not; whose family values education and whose does not.

Researchers John F. Dovidio and Samuel L. Gaertner (2005) have named this phenomenon "aversive racism," and they describe it as qualitatively different from blatant, "old fashioned" racism. Aversive racists sympathize with victims of past injustice, support principles of racial equality, and genuinely regard themselves as nonprejudiced. But, at the same time, they possess conflicting—often unconscious—negative feelings and beliefs about People of Color. The negative feelings that aversive racists have toward People of Color do not reflect open hostility or hatred. Instead, their reactions typically involve discomfort, anxiety, or fear. So, while they find People of Color "aversive," they find any suggestion that they might be prejudiced aversive as well.

The research on aversive racism supports the larger field of study on how implicit bias operates. Via Project Implicit (2011), educators can explore how implicit associations can lead to bias. There are lots of resources available, and we have found Dolly Chugh's *The Person You Mean to Be: How Good People Fight Bias* and Jennifer Eberhardt's *Biased: Uncovering the Hidden Prejudice That Shapes What We See, Think, and Do* to be particularly effective in helping teachers see how their implicit bias may be operating. But while it's important to understand how bias can exist outside our so-called peripheral vision, it's not enough to just know it's there. White teachers need to make a more *explicit* connection to the ways their unexamined bias can get in the way of developing healthy and authentic relationships with Students of Color.

Teacher–Student Relationship Quality (TSRQ)

In *Creating the Opportunity to Learn*, Wade Boykin and Pedro Noguera (2011) examine the racial differences in academic achievement of K–12 students and suggest powerful strategies for challenging institutional barriers to academic success for African American and Latinx students. One strategy is to increase the quality of teacher–student relationships, which they term TSRQ:

1. The degree to which teachers display empathy, support, encouragement, and optimism. (p. 70)
2. The degree to which teachers are perceived to be fair, genuine, and nonpatronizing in their praise and feedback. (p. 70)
3. The degree to which teachers have high expectations for *all* students.

Citing numerous studies, Boykin and Noguera (2011) carefully construct the connection between race, teacher expectations, and student performance. They share a study of middle school students who were asked to self-report who they most want to please with their schoolwork. Approximately 30% of white students said they wanted to please their teacher as opposed to 72% of Black students. The majority of white students ascribed their drive to do well to their own abilities or to their parents. Yet, Black students overwhelmingly cited their teachers, demonstrating the critical importance of positive class interactions and the development of strong, bias-free relationships between white teachers and Students of Color. Now this is not to say that white children do not value or benefit from a strong connection with their teachers. But the sharp statistical difference highlights an important difference: Black students must navigate not only the subject matter but also the possibility that their teacher's perception of their academic ability may be viewed through the lens of racial stereotypes or bias. That prejudice can lead to lower expectations, which can show up in classrooms in the following ways. Teachers:

- call on low-expectation (LE) students less often than on high-expectation (HE) students.
- are likely to give LE students less praise and more criticism for failure.
- show less acceptance of ideas put forth by LE students.
- provide briefer and less informative feedback to questions raised by LE students.
- give LE students less benefit of the doubt.
- allow LE students less time to answer questions.
- are more likely to provide LE students with correct answers, whereas they are more likely to provide clues or rephrase a question for HE students. (Boykin & Noguera, 2011, pp. 78–79)

When we share this data with teachers and school leaders, the first question is always about when the disparity starts. Elementary teachers guess middle school, middle school teachers say ninth grade, and high school teachers say it's more likely to occur in higher education. Yet, Boykin and Noguera (2011) share that TSRQ among *kindergarten* students varies as a function of racial background. Teacher–student interactions were observed across an entire academic year. It was found that white children formed closer, more positive emotional relationships and fewer conflict-ridden relationships with their teachers, and they were more accepted by their classroom peers (as rated by teachers) than were their Black and Latinx peers.

Operationalizing the Research

To help teachers see their implicit racial bias and develop strategies to mitigate the effects, we developed a professional development series based on improving TSRQ. The goal of the East Ed Bias & Relationships Project is to connect academic research to classroom practice to make our teaching more equitable and to strengthen our relationships, especially across racial difference. Using observation data, feedback protocols, and dialogue, we create an opportunity for teachers to self-reflect and to think deeply about their pedagogy as it relates to student engagement. By improving our skills, we make it possible for more children to succeed.

Teachers commit to four to five observations, either in person or via video, over a six-month period. Prior to these observations, teachers will review the tenets of TSRQ and select three or four pedagogical strategies they want to focus on. For example, teachers may invite a colleague to keep track of who they call on during class and what kind of responses they give: do they extend the thinking of some students, but not all? Do they give the answers to some, but invite others into a more critical conversation of their process? Additionally, colleagues can look for patterns of praise and trust or any of the ways that lower expectations might show up in the classroom.

Based on their priorities, teachers will record their lessons, typically in 15–30 minute blocks. Teachers will review the lessons and engage in a feedback session for each observation. These sessions are based on collegial, nonevaluative coaching strategies. One of the most powerful aspects of the project is that teachers take the lead and use the feedback to compare achievement levels across their own gradebook. For example, if a white teacher gets feedback that she continually extends the thinking of her white students but typically gives the right answer to her Students of Color, then she needs to compare that data to her grades. If Students of Color are not achieving at the same level, the teacher has an important data point to work from.

Several themes have emerged from this work with teachers. First, they are so grateful for access to helpful, informative research. To have the data at their fingertips and then to be able to strategize about how they can get better is affirming. So often they are told about problems but not given the resources nor the time to really evolve their teaching, to stop doing harm, and to practice new strategies. Second, they typically don't disaggregate their own classroom data by race. It is important that, in addition to grade-level and school-wide data, teachers are paying attention to achievement patterns in their own classroom. After the project, many teachers continue to use technology, such as Equity Maps https://equitymaps.com/ or EQUIP https://www.equip .ninja/, to help support their data collection. Lastly, they appreciate the collegial work, the time to partner with a fellow practitioner. They can move beyond denial, blame, and shame to support each other to address racial bias and to ensure that they have healthy relationships across the board.

Engaging in Feedback

Another area we do not talk enough about is how our racial background influences the kind of feedback we give to our students. While there have been academic papers and studies about white teacher racial bias and lower expectations for Black students (Boykin & Noguera, 2011; Papageorge, Gershenson, & Min Kang, 2020), we were eager to gather a group of teachers to see if we could identify the role of whiteness in feedback on our own academic assignments. Our central question was: *Do white teachers give different kinds of feedback to their white students than to their Students of Color?*

Working with teachers from two high schools, I (Elizabeth) had 18 participants from the humanities and science departments. Four identified as People of Color, the rest identified as white. Their students were predominantly white, with about a third identifying as

Students of Color. Using three writing assignments (literature analysis, lab report, historical document analysis), we asked teachers to provide a quick summary of the main points of feedback they wanted to give each student on their writing draft during their conference. Teachers met with each student for 3 minutes and recorded their conversation on an iPad. After the student talked with the teacher, we asked the student to tell an observer in their own words what feedback they got on their paper, essentially what they had heard their teacher say in the conference. We then compared what the students said to what the teacher said during the recorded conference.

Here is one example of what a white teacher shared during the conference. The feedback she planned to give to both students was the same: your paper needs more specific and relevant detail. Pay particular attention to the difference in tone between the two conversations. Here's what she said to each student:

> **White teacher to white student:**
> "Jennifer, you have a solid draft here. Your thesis is clear, but you are not providing enough evidence to back it up. You need to cite some specific examples from the text that will support your major claim. Without the evidence, your thesis is just your opinion. Please go back to the text. I want you to revise and submit another draft by the end of the week."

> **White teacher to Student of Color:**
> "Mariah, this is a really great paper. I loved reading it. I really like the way you set up your thesis; it's really on point. I think you could offer some more supporting details, maybe that would help your thesis, but overall, this is really strong. Maybe a few more quotes would help support your claim—but I'm not saying your thesis is off. I hope you will consider submitting a revised draft."

Overall, we noticed that white teachers gave more specific and directed feedback to their white students. They didn't hedge their language, and they seemed very comfortable telling white students exactly what they needed to do to improve their draft. However, when giving feedback to Students of Color (Black students in particular), we noticed that their language became softer, less directed. It was also less specific. And their feedback sounded more like a suggestion than a "must do." This was confirmed by feedback from the students. White students were much more likely to walk away saying, "The teacher said I have to add more specific examples to prove my point." However, Students of Color often reported back, "The teacher really seems to like my draft. They said it was good." When we looked at the notes teachers had provided in advance, they had listed critical feedback for all of their students. Each paper had suggestions for improvement. Yet, the majority of Students of Color reported that a revised draft for them seemed "optional." The overwhelming majority of white students said they were going to revise and submit a new draft. And while the sample size was small, we did not note any difference in the quality of feedback delivered to white students compared to Students of Color by the Teachers of Color; they were consistent with their students across races.

What was perhaps the most interesting outcome of our process was talking with the white teachers about what we noticed. They were adamant that they had given the *same* feedback to all their students, especially since they had written notes for each paper to deliver during the conference. Many were mad at the suggestion that they had exhibited any bias in their feedback. We had to play back the recordings for them to believe us. And their reactions were so telling—many faces turned red, they looked horrified, and some said out loud, "I'm so embarrassed." We asked, "So, how might these disparities in the quality of feedback impact academic achievement?" It was a powerful moment for these teachers, challenging the notion that our grading practices are objective and based on explicit criteria.

The white teachers started putting together the chain of events: So, if my feedback was not good, then my grade on the next draft was not fair because I had not set up my Students of Color for success. In fact, the Students of Color were at a disadvantage compared to the white students. One teacher remarked, "I'm actually favoring my white students and inflating their grades." Many commented that they were afraid that if they were too hard on their Students of Color, they would come across as racist. So, they were hedging their bets: "gentle" feedback meant they would be seen as nice and not racist. But it also meant they were lowering their expectations for their Students of Color. Our small attempt to uncover our bias and the influence of our whiteness on our teaching had yielded major evidence of the role of our race in assessments.

What Comments Really Say

Another area of feedback we were interested in was comment writing, the narratives that some teachers have to write to accompany grade reports. These can take many different forms, but they can all be a place of significant bias if they are not designed well. When I (Elizabeth) was an administrator, I had frequently been tasked with reading over narrative comments to check for consistency and accuracy: Did the teacher have the right name? Are there any grammatical issues? Are all of the sentences clear? But I was not checking for patterns related to race. Were teachers writing different kinds of comments, either in tone or substance, for students of different racial backgrounds? If we did work similar to when we looked at feedback given in writing conferences, could we find any discernible patterns when it came to academic reporting?

Partnering with a colleague at another school, we set up a two-part investigation. I took a sample of narrative comments for grades 9 through 12 and separated them into four groups: white boys, Boys of Color, white girls, and Girls of Color (at the time of the study, we did not have a nonbinary gender category). While I had often read over these narrative comments for an entire grade or for a specific teacher who needed a proofreader, I had never disaggregated them by race and gender. It was interesting to read the comments by cohort group because patterns began to emerge.

Similar to our earlier study of verbal feedback, it was clear in the narrative comments that white students received more specific feedback, especially when it came to what they needed to do to improve their performance in a particular class. Take a look at this narrative for an African American student:

It has been a pleasure having Jannah in class again this year. She is a thoughtful, kind, and conscientious student. She comes to class having spent time working on the problem sets and works well with her peers. In this course students learn by working on problems independently, and then by discussing them as a class. Jannah is engaged in the discussions and takes detailed notes. At times, I am concerned that Jannah is not as vocal as she should be when she has a question. If there is something that she does not understand, I hope she will ask me, either in class or by setting up a time to meet with me outside of class. I look forward to working with Jannah for the remainder of the year.

As you read this over, consider what grade you think Jannah earned. Is there evidence of her mastery? Adequate description of her as a learner? There is one concern expressed about how vocal she is in class, and then a guess that it may be because she doesn't understand. If pressed, what do think Jannah's overall grade was for the semester? She earned a 80% overall, but her final exam grade was 68%. When I first read it, I guessed a B+ for the final grade, and that was a guess because there is really nothing in the narrative that speaks to her mastery of course content. It's striking that there is absolutely no mention of the D+ on her final exam. And this teacher has taught Jannah before; they have a prior relationship. So, why is the feedback so vague and speculative? Might the teacher's expectation for Jannah be 80%, so no need for further improvement—she's doing the best she can?

Here's another narrative for a Black boy:

Paul continues to be an enthusiastic participant in class. While the quality of his work has remained consistent with previous quarters, he has completed all of his work on time. Paul began the quarter playfully interrogating the Chief of Police in our trial project, for which he researched key details he used to shed light on the police's investigation of the accused anarchists. He and a partner delivered a sweeping look at the Civil Rights Movement throughout the twentieth century. While the class did not provide enough time to cover everything they had prepared, it did offer a look at the material we will return to in upcoming months. In several assignments, Paul shows his astute observations and understanding of big concepts. Relying more heavily on facts and taking time to develop his analysis of a concept would improve his work.

There is even less mastery data to go on in this comment than the last one. And the odd passive voice in the last sentence is the only part that even hints at where Paul can improve. He earned a 78% for the class, a C+, but I was hard pressed to decipher what it was about his work that had resulted in that grade besides "more facts" and "more time to develop his analysis." This kind of vague, generalized feedback not only offers little in improvement strategies but also creates a hazy, unfocused snapshot of Paul's work that is even contradictory, as his project showed the use of details (evidence) and analysis of what happened in the trial. If I were a parent reading this, I would think my kid was doing okay. Yet, the final percentage tells a different story. This mixed message echoed what we noticed in the verbal feedback: I have critical feedback, but I'm going to deliver it in a kind of soft, indirect way so you don't think I'm being racist in my feedback. And if my low expectations are being met, there's no real need for specific, directed comments about areas for improvement. We have only shared a few examples here, but over and over, these were types of comments we read for the majority of Students of Color. Yet, most of the white students were given concrete things to do:

You must attend my office hours. Please sign up for a time next week.

We will meet before you hand in your next paper so you can make sure you have addressed all of my suggestions.

If you state a claim, you have to back it up with a specific example or quote from the text.

Interestingly, we did find one white teacher who gave very directed and specific feedback to his Students of Color. Here's an example:

Since writing the new-student report, my concerns about Ignacio's performance have grown. He earned a C on the first major test and 7 out of 20 on the recent quiz. What concerns me most is that I do not see Ignacio taking steps to remedy the situation. Here are some specific suggestions for him: 1) make sure his binder is complete and organized, that it stays that way, and that he brings it to every science class; 2) when working in small groups, stay focused and participate. Stay involved in the work, participate in the conversations, and do not turn towards conversing with other groups; 3) take advantage of the times he and his group present by answering my questions and offering reasons for his answers. These are great one-on-one times for the two of us to identify and correct any misunderstandings on his part, but they are only effective if he participates; 4) come see me outside of class at least once a week to chat about the material. There is plenty of time left for Ignacio to step up and do well in the course.

Although we would caution against the authoritative tone here, ignoring the importance of a learning partnership between student and teacher (Hammond, 2015), this teacher is providing Ignacio with a way forward. The language is concrete, and it is very clear what Ignacio can do to improve his work in the class.

Another trend emerged for students who did not consistently complete the homework assigned: white boys achieved, on average, almost one grade point higher for their overall grade than Black boys. And while both groups demonstrated mastery of course content, achieving at least a B (on average) for quiz and test scores, white boys who didn't do their homework averaged an overall course grade of B while Black boys who didn't do their homework consistently averaged a C. By comparing this data to the TSRQ research and comments from teachers with whom we shared the results, we determined that white boys were more likely to receive the benefit of the doubt when it came to homework. They also were not judged by their lack of homework effort, whereas there were comments about Black boys that linked their lack of homework completion to their effort and/or care for the class. In the narratives, it showed up like this:

White boys:
"Although Chris was not diligent in completing the homework assignments, he did demonstrate consistent mastery on tests and quizzes."

"Steve clearly understands the work we do in class. It would be helpful if he turned in the majority of his homework assignments."

"Mike gets along well with his classmates, and he clearly enjoys the work we do. He's an active participant and asks good questions. While his overall test grade is 87%, his homework grade hovers around 70%."

Black boys:

"I am concerned about Eric's work ethic. While he is active in class and participates when called on, he has only completed a few of the homework assignments. His refusal to get those assignments done is having an adverse effect on his grade."

"On several occasions I have reminded Jason to turn in his work, but he is unwilling to get his homework problems completed. To be a successful student, he must be willing to complete all assignments."

"Brian has not attended any office hours, and the majority of the time he shows up to class having not completed the homework assignment. He needs to demonstrate more care and consideration for his work and his classmates."

Notice how much judgment there is? What is simply an observation for the white students becomes an indictment for the Black students, like they are intentionally disobeying the teacher's authority. The last one is particularly harsh as it directly calls into question the student's care not only for himself, but for others. How does this kind of assumption help to improve learning?

For part two of our inquiry, my colleague, Mariama Richards, met with student cohort groups to talk about how they experienced teacher written feedback as well as their academic performance. She met with students by grade level, racial background, and gender identity. She noticed that the students parroted the comments they had received from teachers. It was as if the narratives in their grade reports were internalized to become part of the way they saw themselves as students.

Assessing for Equity

This study revealed many larger concerns about grading practices in general. Given the lack of correlation between achievement and homework practices, especially for grades K through 5, why were teachers weighing homework grades so much? (Vatterott, 2018). And what about class participation—how were teachers deciding what "good participation" was? We then turned our attention to working with teachers on what is considered the "third rail" of education: grades.

Given all the time and emphasis devoted to grading student performance, it is shocking how little time is actually devoted to talking about these practices in schools and how race and racism can impact assessment. Part of this is because most teachers believe their practices are objective. How often have we said or heard, "I didn't *give* you a grade; you *earned* it." Additionally, the way we grade is directly connected to our values and belief of who we are as teachers and what we think the purpose of grades is. So, it can be a quagmire, but one that is worth the fight because there is so much inequity and room for improvement.

The first step is to help teachers understand why their practices are not as objective as they think. Texts such as Joe Feldman's *Grading for Equity: What It Is, Why It Matters, and How It Can Transform Schools and Classrooms* is a great place to start. Along with our colleague Lori Cohen, we facilitate a multisession review of Feldman's research and the scholarship of other educators who are looking explicitly at their grading practices through an antibias lens. Our purpose is to shift cultures of assessment to have more equitable outcomes for students. Monthly sessions meet over the course of the semester/school year so that practitioners can be reviewing and adapting their assessment practices in real time via collegial cohorts. For example, participants:

- receive a strong foundation for the theoretical underpinnings of assessing for equity;
- dig into common assessment practices and complete equity checks: exploding mythologies, rethinking approaches;
- receive tools and practices for classroom and self-assessment;

- examine equitable assessment practices through social, emotional, and academic lenses;
- investigate bias and its impact on student assessment;
- transfer learning to create new, more equitable practices; and
- activate leadership and shift perspectives within teams and school sites.

The resistance to this kind of work is not to be underestimated. When we first started facilitating these academic conversations, many white teachers told us they were offended. How dare we assume they had bias in their grading! Didn't we know what good teachers they are? We started by looking at the research on homework efficacy. Even asking questions (What value does homework have? Do we know it impacts learning? For whom?) was enough to put teachers on the defensive. Again, it became very clear that most teachers had been told to assign homework, but very few had considered what effective homework is. In most teacher education programs, it is a footnote, and once we could get teachers past their initial responses, it became clear that there was much to discuss and learn. The purpose and creation of rubrics was another area where teachers could see how making their expectations explicit would mitigate bias. We even encouraged them to think about cocreating assessment rubrics with their students. Connecting our antiracist work explicitly to grading also helped teachers see that practices to make our schools more racially just are also effective teaching strategies across the board.

More Remedies

With the work and words of Lisa Delpit in our minds, we must make the implicit *explicit* so that systems of power are rendered visible, especially for those who have been underserved by our educational practices. As teachers, we must make our own beliefs, attitudes, and practices more explicit.

The first step is to understand how stereotypes that are operating may impact the expectations we have for particular students. The TSRQ project helps to connect the dots so teachers really know how *identity threat* may be operating in their classroom. Dr. Claude Steele (2011) coined this term during his time at Stanford University when he noticed that his African American students, who had been at the top of their high school classes, were not doing as well academically as their prior achievements had predicted. He first thought it was an issue of self-esteem, but he then realized these students were experiencing *stereotype threat*: the threat of being viewed through the lens of a negative stereotype or the fear of doing something that would inadvertently confirm a stereotype. In this case, the stereotype was that they had only gotten into Stanford because they were Black. So, they had to work overtime to prove to their professors and peers that they deserved to be there. And that constant identity stress has consequences. Students living with identity threat become hyper aware of their performance, and they experience ongoing stress responses that can significantly impact their ability to do their work, such as by sapping their working memory capacity and by affecting executive functioning skills. And students who need to constantly monitor their environment for racial threat experience frequent amygdala responses—freeze, flight, or fight— which further impede their ability to learn.

The good news is that the impact of stereotype threat can be dramatically reduced when teachers make their expectations explicit. When a student knows what the grading criteria are, they don't have to guess the reason why they got a bad grade (e.g., "my teacher doesn't like me"). They can see that they didn't fulfill the expectations and recognize what they can do to improve their performance.

Zaretta's Hammond's WISE feedback protocol can help teachers ensure that their approach to assessment supports many of the antiracist strategies we have detailed here:

1. An explicit holding of high standards
2. A personal assurance that students are capable and can improve with effort
3. Specific, actionable steps to work on

First, teachers must have high expectations for all students and challenge any stereotypes or prejudice that may be getting in the way.

Second, they need to build authentic relationships with students that are demonstrate true care for student success. If they have taken a colorblind or color-evasive stance, they need to see how that can increase racism because they are ignoring relevant student experiences and identities that are connected to learning. Students need to know their teachers have their backs and are committed to their growth and development. Finally, our feedback must give students a clear path forward, with detailed instructions on what they need to do to meet expectations and the steps to get there.

CASE STUDY: BIAS AND FEEDBACK

You are finishing up a conference with a Black student. You feel that your feedback has been spot on, and from your perspective, the conversation has gone well. As you are wrapping up, you notice your student's facial expression has changed, and you ask how the student feels the conference went. They say, "Whatever. It's all the same. There's no way I can get a better grade because you've already decided I can't write this. You haven't liked me from the start, and I'm pretty sure I know why."

Small Group Scenario Questions (each person answers)

- In ONE WORD, what's your immediate reaction to the scenario?
- Has anyone experienced this or a similar situation?
- How prepared do you feel to address this situation?
- How would you respond?

CHAPTER 7

Developing an Antiracist Leadership Practice

In this chapter, we will detail how white administrators, and those with other kinds of leadership responsibilities, can develop specific strategies to work more effectively at dismantling racism. This includes building more authentic and principled relationships with Leaders of Color, who are often severely underrepresented on leadership teams. We will also look at governance structures, such as school boards, and their role in supporting antiracist practices.

School leaders are in a unique position to address racism on campus, but many are not sure where to start. A revised version of a letter that one school leader sent to their entire faculty and staff is instructive. The original version of this letter was in response to a 90-minute professional development session for a predominantly white school, led by a white antiracist educator who described all the advantages that whiteness had afforded her and how she was taking steps to challenge racism:

Dear Faculty and Staff,
Thank you for attending and giving feedback on last week's professional development meeting. From your feedback, most of you felt the presenter's personal story, and her presentation generally, helped make you more aware of and/or more understanding of white identity and the history of race in the US.

Yet when it came to the presenter's use of specific language related to racial advantage, such as her description of white supremacy, many of you felt that her discussion was not useful because it seemed inconsistent and perhaps confusing, given the way our community talks about race.

While we need to continue to develop ways for students to understand their identity, we need to do this in a way that all students can participate. Unfortunately, we have heard from both students of color and white students that they have experienced anxiety when teachers have used the term "white privilege" in their lessons. It seems that some of these more complex concepts are not being broken down in ways that ensure all of our students are learning to their full potential. Putting the students first, I challenge the use of this convenient but loaded rhetoric and ask that you avoid using the terms "white privilege" and "white supremacy" in your classes.

I know that you all want to do what's best for your students. I also recognize the value of freedom of expression and acknowledge that changing how we talk with students may be difficult for many of us. Of course, I am open to continued feedback and dialogue around this topic. Please let me know if you would like to discuss this further.

Moving From Protecting the Comfort of White People to Building Antiracist Skills

This model letter illustrates how school leaders often sabotage efforts to challenge racism, whether intentionally or not. Here is a school that clearly wanted to do some important work together, but as soon as it got hard or messy or uncomfortable, they decided to start banning words. As we have pointed out, the language is not really the issue. Yes, terms like "white privilege" and "white supremacy" can be hard for some students and adults (see Curriculum Suggestion: A Note About White Privilege in Chapter 5), but they are hardly just rhetorical. They describe the ways that whiteness works as a system, and it is true that both white students and Students of Color can experience discomfort. But does banning the terms end the stress? And for whom? This positions a symptom as the disease, and as a result, the entire conversation gets shut down.

Here's what this leader could have done to both address this leader's concerns *and* keep the skill-building going:

1. Disaggregate the feedback to the presentation by race. Knowing that less than a majority said the presentation around language was useful, we should ask:
    a. How many white staff/faculty said that? Are there any other markers we need for more fully interpreting the data, such as tenure at the school and in the profession, gender identity?
    b. What do we mean by "useful"? To whom? In service of what?

The feedback in this illustration is used as proof of an issue, and the blunt tool of "don't say these words" is the white-silence remedy. But it's not really clear what this data is saying. So, when gathering feedback, make sure your questions are specific. If you want to know about student learning, then ask about that. And be sure to disaggregate feedback when talking about racism.

2. Contradictory messages are a hallmark of white supremacy: do this work, but don't really do this work. Or, do it with one hand tied behind your back. The leader in this illustration recognizes that this is a complicated issue. So, don't respond to complexity by banning two terms. It's like the three-strikes rule applied to school discipline or like zero tolerance. Those kinds of statements are evidence of further avoidance for change, which means the status quo remains firmly in place. It's not antiracism; it's the prioritization of white people's comfort over the impact of racism on Students and Faculty/Staff of Color.

3. Clearly, some students and adults have let the leader in this illustration know that there are conversations about racism that are happening that are causing significant upset. So, focus on *that* feedback. Where is it happening? In particular classes? With particular teachers? Let's create a culture of feedback where these concerns can be both raised and addressed *as they happen*. Sure, we have seen white teachers use the term "white privilege" to get white kids to think about systems of advantage, and sometimes

it can feel heavy handed. White students will express feelings of guilt and shame. And that may make things harder for some Students of Color who then have those feelings to manage on top of the racism they endure. But, again, *banning the term doesn't interrupt the bigger pattern.* Whether you use the term "white privilege" or not, we know that significant numbers of students *already* feel shame and guilt about racism. And if they don't have a place to reconcile those feelings, they will fester whether you call it "white supremacy" or not. So, let's get curious about better ways to have those conversations:

a. Do some teachers need to do the work the presenter was suggesting? How can they model the exploration of their own white identity like the speaker did? Who could help mentor faculty/staff?

b. Do teachers need help facilitating these conversations? Do they need to practice with each other? Get tips? Guidelines? Support for curriculum development?

c. Would affinity spaces be useful to reduce harm in cross-racial settings?

d. What would it mean to hold faculty/staff accountable for the development of these skills so it's not just an "opt in" or "I-can-do-it-if-I-deem-it-useful" moment? How could school leaders assess teachers on their skill development?

In addition to inviting more conversation, as the leader in this illustration did, set up time and space for more professional development to focus on a scope and sequence for introducing the terms. Sounds like the presenter did her job. How could you model a similar process for students?

As teachers are developing their skills, school leaders need to support and scaffold their development. Too often, leaders don't have the knowledge, feedback, and accountability skills they need to implement antiracist practices. They also may be facing resistance from powerful people that they don't know how to navigate or that they just don't want to confront for fear of jeopardizing their job. In either event, leaders are often not well-positioned to support systemic change. Another disturbing trend we see is the one Administrator of Color on a team is put in charge of "diversity work" whether or not they have the skill and expertise to lead racial equity work. Often these administrators are set up for failure from the beginning: they are given no real power to make change, no budget, and no support when there is resistance and pushback.

Designing Effective Professional Development

School leaders need to be at the helm of ensuring antiracist, systemic change. Whether a superintendent, head of school, principal, or department chair, anyone in a leadership position must be able to clearly articulate the purpose and the vision for change and must be vigilant in monitoring for impact and evaluating for effectiveness.

Here we return to the WhAT questions (*wh*ite *a*ntiracist *t*eaching) we first shared in the introduction. The WhAT framework can assist leadership in their efforts to effectively anticipate, respond, evaluate, and plan for future antiracist work. There is no shortage of information about the ways in which racism is operating. So, the process is about developing the skills, the *will*, and the stamina to confront racism and about being ready for the inevitable pushback. Any time you want to change the status quo, there will be resistance. But leaders often roll out new initiatives without carefully considering where the pushback will come from and what they can do to get out in front of it. They cross their fingers and hope it will all be okay, but hope is not a strategy. Dr. Jamie Washington talks about reframing resistance as the energy needed for change as opposed to seeing it as the enemy that is getting in the way. People only resist what they care about, so how can we be prepared to address concerns and feedback regarding our antiracist efforts when we are challenged on what we know is best for our students? The Elevator Pitch activity we outlined in Chapter 3 is a great example of anticipating and responding to resistance. Leaders need to be prepared to stand up for their antiracist initiatives and programs, not in a defensive way but in a way that connects the dots to research, data, methods, and, most importantly, student experiences. And there are always people who are not going to agree (we'll talk more about white parents

114 Learning and Teaching While White

in the next chapter). So, prioritize the impact on the most affected students, get savvy about who's resisting change and why, and build coalitions of constituents who want to transform school communities.

These questions can provide a kind of road map that can help leadership create an antiracist scope and sequence for your own context, in any school or district.

WhAT Questions: What should I be asking myself, my colleagues, my students, and my school?

1. How does racial diversity in a classroom support learning outcomes? (Value of racial difference)
2. How do we come to understand what it means to be white? (Racial identity development)
3. What gets in the way of healthy racial identity development? (System of racism/internalized dominance)
4. Where and how do racist attitudes, language, and behavior show up in schools? (Identification and data)
5. How do we address racial stereotypes and racism? (Skill development)
6. How can we create and model antiracist pedagogy and curricula? (Teaching/coaching practices)

Here each area is explored in greater detail.

1. How does racial diversity in a classroom support learning outcomes? (Value of racial difference)

Most schools express a commitment to racial diversity, but do they really understand why having racially diverse classrooms makes *all* students smarter? (See Chapter 3, Elevator Pitch exercise for how to develop this skill.) Professors at the University of Michigan have provided significant research on this important topic. Dr. Scott Page wrote *The Difference: How the Power of Diversity Creates Better Groups, Firms, Schools, and Societies* to illustrate how diverse teams enhance and improve collaboration as well as outcomes. And Gurin et al. (2002) have been able to quantify the value of racial diversity in classrooms and on campuses across the country.

Gurin et al. (2002) looked at informal interactions among African American, Asian American, Latinx, and white students as well as at classroom environments. Their purpose was to measure the effects, if any, of racial diversity on academic and social growth. They identified learning outcomes, such as intellectual engagement, self-confidence, the drive to achieve, academic skills, writing and listening abilities, general knowledge, analytic and problem-solving skills, and the ability to think and write critically, to measure learning. They also considered democracy outcomes, such as the ability of students to participate in an increasingly heterogeneous democracy. To participate fully, students need to understand and consider multiple perspectives, to appreciate common values, and to understand and accept cultural differences that arise in a racially and ethnically diverse community.

Gurin et al. (2002) found that all four groups of students were positively impacted by both informal and classroom interactions with racially diverse peers. Many educators have argued that diversity can be achieved without the presence of racial diversity. Since content about race can be introduced in classrooms, it was important for the researchers to explore whether informal interaction among peers had significant effects on learning. The researchers found that informal interaction with racially diverse peers had the greatest effect on learning and democracy outcomes, confirming the value and necessity for racially diverse student populations. The most consistent effects were found for white students. Both classroom diversity and informal interaction were significantly related to intellectual engagement for this group. And Students of Color benefitted most when they were not the only, or one of a few, representative of their particular ethnic group. Overall, the learning and democracy outcomes for all four groups were positively affected by interaction with racially diverse peers both in and out of the classroom setting. Thus, a diverse student body is clearly a resource and a necessary condition for engagement with diverse peers and for the attainment of academic goals.

When we have the opportunity to learn side by side with someone who is different from us, we experience cognitive dissonance. We bump up against something new and unfamiliar, and then we have to push through our discomfort to reach a new understanding—what teachers refer to as the learning moment. That dissonance promotes critical thinking: "That's a different way of looking at that. I never thought of it that way. I wonder what it means?" This is why the white students showed the most growth and development: schools are often the first, and perhaps the only, integrated spaces that white students experience, given the effects of discrimination and neighborhood segregation. While most Students of Color often have to navigate multiracial spaces, many white students can spend most of their time avoiding interactions with or apart from interacting with People of Color. So, while this does not mean we should educate white students about race on the backs of Students of Color, it does indicate that efforts to create more equitable and racially integrated schools benefit both Students of Color and white students by increasing critical engagement and opportunities for authentic collaboration.

2. How do we come to understand what it means to be white? (Racial identity development)

As we noted in Chapter 1, the work to make our schools more antiracist starts with ourselves. When working with aspiring school leaders, the first question we pose is: How does your identity impact your leadership? It can be very challenging for principal candidates to answer this question, and many say, "I've never really thought about this." Most have considered their gender, but the vast majority of white educators have only a surface-level understanding of their whiteness. We spend considerable time connecting issues of racial identity with topics like hiring, coaching, supervision, and evaluation. Leaders need to recognize their own positionality and to be explicit about the ways their race affects how they lead the institution.

3. What gets in the way of healthy racial identity development? (System of racism/internalized dominance)

Effective antiracist leaders understand how racism operates at all levels, including institutional practices, policies, and procedures—the areas of school that are largely systematized. These are the big places where power is often wielded outside of the classroom: course tracking and enrollment in honors/AP classes; discipline; grading standards and policies; hiring; evaluation of staff/faculty; budget allocations; and staffing numbers. Often, racism is described in only personal or inter-personal terms—the old "one bad apple" argument. But racism oper-ates on all levels. Leaders need to analyze how the way we do things in schools is derived from deeply racist stereotypes, from prejudices, and from the founding of schools as sorting mechanisms—who's smart and who's not—and tools of segregation.

4. Where and how do racist attitudes, language, and behavior show up in schools? (Identification and data)

We have noticed many schools that are now proclaiming themselves to be "antiracist." Yet when we ask these schools to name where racism is currently operating so they know exactly what they need to address in their antiracist practice, we get one of two answers. The first is usually a long pause with no real response. The other is usually some kind of uncomfortable or defensive response: "Well, we don't want to dwell on the negative. We want to be proactive in our approach." The problem is you can't develop an antiracist practice if you are not absolutely clear on where, when, and how racism is showing up at school. You can't dismantle something you can't effectively name.

5. How do we address racial stereotypes and racism? (Skill development)

So often, we position the work to challenge racism as something innate to certain teachers. Sort of like, "Miguel is really good at having these conversations with those kids. He just seems to connect with them." We act like fighting racism is something you're born with—usually dependent on your racial background—instead of recognizing it as a set of skills we can *all* learn. White leaders often assume that Teachers of Color will just "naturally" include racial diversity in their curricu-lum. This is a dangerous assumption for many reasons:

1. it continues to locate race as biological (innate) and thus a deter-minant of how certain people will behave, and this perpetuates racist assumptions and stereotypes;
2. although People of Color experience racism, it doesn't mean

they all have the skills and knowledge to challenge it in their practice; and

3. it presumes antiracism is *not* the work of white teachers, so there are no expectations for white teachers to up their skills and affords them lots of excuses for why they can't learn how to talk about race and to challenge racism.

Once again, there's teaching, and then there's teaching about race—and those two things are not seen as connected. Effective school leaders recognize the need for antiracist skill development. They layer this work into every aspect of school culture, and they commit significant time and resources to making sure their teachers and fellow administrators have the skills required to be both excellent and antiracist, for one cannot exist without the other.

6. How can we create and model antiracist pedagogy and curricula? (Teaching/coaching practices)

Chapter 5 details many of the moves teachers can make toward antiracism, and leaders need to create the space for this development to happen. If it is a priority at the administrative table, it will be a priority for the school. Most importantly, white leaders must be transparent about their own work and model for their colleagues and community the ways they are developing their antiracist practice. This is especially critical when considering cross-racial supervision. They need to support teachers in the face of resistance, especially when parents are questioning curricular shifts. They must be willing to speak to the value of racial diversity and equity in clear and certain ways. They need to be accountable for harm that has been done, whether in the past or under their watch, and they need to offer a vision for the road forward.

Principled Partnerships Across Race

It can be challenging to find effective cross-racial connections among leaders. Most Administrators of Color report that their relationships with their fellow white team members are at best superficial and at worst explicitly racist. Most diversity-related efforts focus on curriculum and instruction, which we need desperately. But we also need people in positions of authority who can effectively coach and evaluate classroom teachers and staff. And they need to have positive relationships with their Colleagues of Color. Currently, the racial makeup of administrators mirrors teachers; about 78% of principals identify as white. That means white supremacy will be alive and well at the administrative level, and around other leadership tables, unless schools are taking explicit steps to interrupt patterns of dominance that emerge when whiteness lines up with institutional power and authority.

So, what are some of the things administrators need to be aware of to be better antiracist leaders? I (Elizabeth) had the opportunity to serve as a codirector with a Woman of Color for 10 years. We were hired at the same time and had the opportunity to really develop our leadership practice together. But there were a few key assumptions we had to address at the beginning of our tenure:

1. There is a historical tension between white women and Women of Color that has evolved over centuries due to enslavement, racism, and the failure of feminism to truly include the lived realities and experiences of Women of Color in meaningful and nuanced ways. We agreed to be honest about those forms of oppression and how they might show up in our relationship so we would be able to work through them.

2. We agreed to raise these issues with each other privately whenever possible. We called this our "no daylight" rule. Publicly, we knew we had to present a unified front as much as possible. First, we were new, and that is always an opportunity for racism to wreak its havoc. We could be blamed or dismissed for any issues due to the fact that we were "new around here" and thus not qualified to make change. So, our work had to be *tight*. Second, we knew colleagues would try to pit us against each other, the old divide and conquer. So, when someone started to complain to me about my codirector's work (or vice versa) we were quick to say, "Thank you for the feedback. Let's get all three of us in the room so we can talk through the concern you are raising." Third, we were committed to addressing tensions privately so we could

work through them on our time and in a productive way—and not in front of our colleagues. An additional consideration was the fact that there are so few models of productive cross-racial dialogue that any perceived conflict between us (real or imagined) would be exploited in the service of racism by white people who didn't want to be challenged or questioned, "See, she won't even trust Elizabeth." But the no daylight rule was not an agreement to endure repeated harm. If these mistakes continued after we tried to work through it, we were committed to engaging in a different process to address it.

3. One year we had the opportunity to be coached by Enid Lee, an antiracist professional development specialist and writer, and she said to us, "Assume racism is operating until proven otherwise." It is probably one of our most valuable leadership tenets. And it has served us well over the years because white leaders usually start from the opposite pole: they assume racism is *not* operating until proven otherwise.

It was clear that if my codirector said certain things, she would be dismissed. But if I said the same thing, I was heard. We were strategic and leveraged our positionality to be as effective as possible. We spoke openly with our boss, a white man, about what we noticed, and he helped us think about both our roles and his in advancing particular initiatives. In a way, we colluded and conspired against racism. We leveraged our racial difference in a positive way to think about how we could expand our circle and bring in more allies. And we laughed a lot, which really helped. There was a deep sense of caring for each other, for our shared antiracist work, and for the children and families we had pledged to serve. Most importantly, we knew we were better together.

In coaching cross-racial teams, it's important to start with the ways race, and other salient identifiers, might be showing up in our shared work. We consider how feedback styles are influenced by racial backgrounds; how approaches to problems and comfort with conflict can be impacted by our identity. By being clear about who we are and what we value, we can then develop authentic partnerships. But if race is unacknowledged and we aren't actively talking about how it impacts our leadership styles and strategies, we are in big trouble. Not only will we be less effective, but we will also ensure that racism will continue to operate unheeded.

FOCUS QUESTIONS: ANTIRACIST POLICY AND PROCEDURE PROTOCOL

How can leaders ensure a comprehensive look at practices, policies, and procedures that may inadvertently, or knowingly, lead to exclusion or inequity among students, teachers/staff, and families? No policy is too minor to examine. Racism is insidious and often concealed in the seemingly small details. Here are some questions to use to start to interrogate policies, procedures, and practices (abbreviated as "practices" below) to uncover how racism may be operating and indicate areas for change, deletion, and/or further inquiry. These questions were inspired by the work of Paul Gorski (2019) in his article, "Avoiding Racial Equity Detours."

1. How might this practice get in the way of racial equity? How might racism be operating?
2. How might this practice support the myth of meritocracy?
3. Who are the groups or people who get left out or marginalized by this practice?
4. What do we need in order to make change to that practice and to the underlying ideologies to make it equitable?
5. Do we have the institutional will and the resources to make a meaningful change to this practice?
6. Do we have all the information and resources we need to take action?
7. Do the changes to this practice address the root of the inequity, or does it mask the inequity by just "celebrating" (not affirming) diversity or reinforcing tropes or stereotypes?
8. What steps can we take to ensure that marginalized groups participate in the decision-making process, ensuring that no one person is asked to represent an entire racial group or demographic?

9. Is there a process for the least powerful and most impacted to evaluate the success of this practice?
10. Does the pace and plan for change prioritize the comfort and interests of people who have the least interest in that progress?

Revise those policies and practices right now. Then attend to the dynamics of institutional culture that resulted in the existence of biased policies to begin with.

—Paul Gorski (2019, p. 60)

How Whiteness Impacts the Recruitment and Retention of Teachers/Staff of Color

Black and Latinx teachers are the least likely to stay once they enter the workforce compared to their white colleagues, according to the 2016 State of Racial Diversity in the Educator Workforce by the US Department of Education (Policy and Program Studies Service Office of Planning, Evaluation, and Policy Development, 2016). And many white leaders seem surprised by this fact. The other statement we hear again and again is that schools would hire more Teachers of Color, "but they just can't find any." This begs the question: Where are you looking? Over the years, we have developed networks for hiring and recruiting Teachers of Color, and here are some of our lessons learned.

After the *Brown v. Board of Education of Topeka* decision in 1954, districts were forced to integrate their students. But they fired most of the Black teachers. It was alright for white and Black children to be together, but the deep racism of the time would not be okay with Black teachers working with white children. This brutal reality is at the root of why we don't have more Teachers of Color: we lost an entire generation of Black teachers and sent a clear message that they need not apply. And unless we are willing to make more changes, they will continue to be underrepresented and to leave our schools when they just can't take the racism anymore.

So, we really need to be clear about why the teaching core is over-whelmingly white and stop acting like this has something to do with scarcity. Teachers of Color enter the profession for the same reasons white people do: professional growth, support of young people, desire to make change, love of learning and knowledge, etc. So, let's make sure our institutions are promoting development of all our profession-als by rooting out where white supremacy may be influencing the ways we hire, retain, and fire Teachers of Color.

We can start by creating job descriptions that include racial liter-acy in the expectations. When leading a candidate search, the criteria for selection need to be explicit and documented in a rubric whenever possible. Without this, there is more room for bias and a greater chance that we will choose the candidate who makes us feel more comfortable or who seems to have the right "fit," often a code word for "one of us." If other staff will be involved in the interviewing process, they need to be trained on the ways that interviewer bias can show up. They need to understand how stereotype threat works. Administrators also need to collect hiring data to see what the patterns are: Why is it that we have People of Color as finalists, but they never get the jobs? How might racial bias be operating in our process? And be sure to look at discipline and firing data too. Is there a racialized pattern there too?

We know that hiring managers will self-replicate unless they have specific hiring goals and procedures to interrupt racial bias. They respond to things on a resume that feel familiar and question or dis-regard professional experience or affiliations they don't know or value. So, paying attention to how their identity can influence important decisions is critical in our efforts to increase both the recruitment and retention of People of Color. Just as we looked at the impact of racial identity on feedback teachers give to students in Chapter 6, how might the feedback they give to a peer change based on race? How might race impact a supervisory relationship? Asking candidates to consider these questions *before* assuming administrative positions ensures that understanding racial identity will be viewed as central to great leader-ship. And it will be extended to the work they do when hiring others.

One school we worked with found that there had been a series of Black people who had been let go from a particular department after only 2 to 3 years. There was always "a good reason" for the termination, but when they dug a little deeper, they realized that the issue in each case was around feedback. Managers had *said* they had given clear messages about how each employee needed to improve, but they reported not seeing enough "growth." So, the school wondered, what was the quality of the feedback given? Was it always communicated by a white supervisor? Maybe it wasn't just the employee's fault. Might the supervisor have been vague or indirect? And then they asked, are there current white staff who have also been given feedback, have not really applied it, and who are still employed? Not surprisingly, there were. So, why were they okay with white mediocrity?

On a final note regarding retention, leaders need to be well aware of the "tax" (King, 2016) levied on Teachers of Color: their unrecognized and unpaid labor that results from our inability to effectively deal with racism. This tax is comprised of all the ways they have to compensate for our lack of skill and knowledge: a Latinx teacher who has to translate for a parent because the system didn't recognize the need; the few Teachers of Color who are asked to serve on every equity committee; Teachers of Color who are always asked to talk to Students of Color when there is an issue because they "have a better relationship with those kids." By putting extra burdens on these teachers, we not only contribute to their burnout and experiences of racism, we also leave structural gaps—like not having consistent translation services—unaddressed, which continues the cycle of underserving Families of Color.

Faculty Meetings:
Where All (Antibias) Dreams Go to Die

Weekly or monthly meetings with all staff are an amazing opportunity to build community and skills that facilitate greater equity, but they are often underutilized or used to communicate what could have been conveyed in an email. Leaders need to see meeting times as *precious resources not to be squandered.* Like any great classroom lesson, they need to be planned and designed with key learning points in mind. And they need to be organized in such a way that they will disrupt predictable racist patterns. For example, too many meetings feature a school leader standing at the head of the room with all staff and faculty seated in front of them. The leader offers up a new initiative and then asks the larger group: "So, what do you all think about this?" As if scripted, the same three hands go up, usually all white people. Those same white responders will begin to debate with each other, adding a "devil's advocate" scenario, to which another white person vehemently objects. An entire discussion can grind to a halt while the white people fight among themselves and demand "more clarification on the terms being used." We have seen ironic Bingo cards circulating on social media that reflect these predictable patterns, indicating the presence of a system at work. As part of his graduate work, our colleague William Yepes-Amaya researched whose voice was typically heard and found that generally Teachers of Color only speak if presenting (Yepes-Amaya, 2019). Yepes-Amaya notes the regularity of white people pretending to ask a question when they really are making statements or promoting work they are doing. We have witnessed white colleagues talking over and taking credit for work done by Teachers of Color. And there are usually two or three white people on the periphery of the meeting, often men, who are clearly not involved in what is going on. They are busy grading papers, staring out the window, and mostly communicating that they have no obligation nor interest in contributing. Ultimately, all these behaviors reflect a jockeying for power, and leaders can short-circuit the entire mess before it gets started.

Consider alternative ways to gather staff feedback, such as collecting information or feedback in advance, giving colleagues time to write their reflections during the meeting, breaking people up into small groups to discuss an issue, discussing a shared reading on a particular topic you want considered. We often start a faculty meeting with an example of an antiracist lesson, so a different teacher or grade level/ subject area shares each time and walks us through (or does) a lesson with the group. This shared practice not only strengthens relationships between teachers, it also gives them time to ask each other questions and learn more about their practice. And whenever you watch someone else, you reflect on your *own* process, promoting self-reflection at the same time.

Department Chairs as Gatekeepers:
Is That Really the Job You Want?

Here is a case study from a few high school science departments we worked with. In looking at their student enrollment data, they noticed that Black and Latinx students were severely underrepresented in honors and AP science classes. For years, they had lamented this fact, but they had just sort of resigned themselves to it being the way it was—and were quick to say the issue started in middle school, so what could they do about it? We started by looking at the prerequisites for enrolling in their courses. They had an elaborate list of so-called "objective measures" for granting approval, which was at the department chair's ultimate discretion. As we worked through their list, they saw how much subjectivity and bias there was in their process. And the department chairs hated having to fight with kids and parents about their placement. All of them said it was one of the worst parts of their jobs. They also noticed that the vast majority of parents who called and advocated for their children to get into the higher level classes were—you guessed it—white. And we asked, "Do you really want to be a gatekeeper?" The answer was a resounding "no."

Based on their reflections, they made some critical shifts:

1. Instead of saying students had to have "departmental approval" to register, they let anyone sign up for AP/Honors who wanted to take the class. If there were particular students they had concerns about (e.g., based on a previous grade in a similar course), they made appointments to talk with the student and their parent/ caregiver. They addressed any concerns head on, made the course expectations explicit, and detailed the work they would need to see, such as:

   By the sixth week of class,

   • You need to have a B average.
   • All due work must have been submitted.
   • You must be following the class participation guidelines.
   • You must have attended at least one office hour session.

If any of these criteria were not met, the plan was to convene the group and talk about next steps and any additional support they needed to put in place. Subsequently, even the teachers reported that the clarification of their expectations and clear delineation of what students needed to do had really helped them be more consistent in their assessment practice.

2. Instead of just making a blanket statement to students that they should "apply for an AP class if you want," they started approaching and talking with Students of Color, one by one, about why they thought it was a good idea for the student to register for the course. Echoing the TSRQ study data we shared in Chapter 6, these teachers were developing stronger relationships with these students and working to challenge any stereotype threat that might have been operating.

These changes yielded big results. Over the next couple of years, they saw the numbers of Students of Color in upper-level classes double. Those students were successful, and the department chairs were way more fulfilled in their jobs. The other conversation this opened up was "Why did we need to have leveled courses at all? (See research we share in Chapter 8 for more on the myths around tracking students by ability.)

The Role of School Boards and Trustees

Understanding how antiracist work can function at the governance level has been a challenge for many boards. While their sphere of influence is not day-to-day operations, they make significant decisions that affect schools and their ability to challenge racism every day. Here we will break down their major responsibilities and how their time and resources can be leveraged to support antiracism.

1. Hiring, retaining, and evaluating the superintendent/head of school:

- Are antiracist expectations clear for these school leaders? Are they evaluated on their antiracist practice? Are they given the time and money to manage antiracist programs and training? Are they supported in their antiracist work by the school board?

2. Keepers of the mission and values of the district/school, including curricular adoptions and school schedules:

- Does the mission include support for racial equity? Do the values reflect that commitment? Are they explicit or implicit? When the school board is reviewing a new curricular adoption, who is around the table?

3. Fiduciary responsibilities, the cost of inequity:

- Have school board members received training around antibias education? Do they understand the impact of racism on the district/school? Are they reviewing relevant and disaggregated data? How are community members and stakeholders involved with school board decisions?

Board Composition and Pipelines

According to Nonprofit Quarterly, boards look very similar to the teaching force (Dovidio & Gaertner, 2005). They are about 85% white with about 90% of board chairs identifying as white. Many boards have articulated the need to have more Board Members of Color, but it can feel like this is just a numbers game. They want to recruit People of Color, yet are they really considering what they need to shift to effectively retain and benefit from different perspectives? And if they bring on new Board Members of Color, are they willing to take their feedback? Boards run the risk of repeating the same old patterns of racial inequality if they don't look carefully at their current culture and ways of operating that replicate white supremacy. Similar to what we see in hiring, the recruitment of new board members can often operate like an old boys' network: we rely on our connections and often don't look beyond our immediate circles, which means we will just bring on more white people. So, what's happening to disrupt business as usual? We need to think more expansively about our pipeline to leadership: Brainstorm ways to recruit more Families of Color to get involved as class parents or serve in the leadership of the PTA, as those roles are great stepping-stones to becoming more involved.

Final Thoughts

There is no shortage of things that demand our attention as school leaders; there are always fires to put out. But without a broad view and vigilance to keep racial equity at the fore, schools quickly get absorbed back into the system of racism that is designed to maintain itself. Leadership requires creativity and the ability to think beyond what we know. School leaders need to stay focused on a vision of what is possible, not just what is probable. We must also inspire and infuse that vision into every aspect of the school community. Only then will schools start to outrun the moving walkway of racial oppression. Only then will we have schools that are actually and intentionally serving all students.

CASE STUDIES FOR LEADERSHIP

When analyzing these case studies:

1. Identify the problem(s) in the case study.
2. Articulate the different perspectives. Who is not at the table?
3. Consider possible challenges/resistance and opportunities for change.
4. What would be an equitable outcome? What information do you still need?
5. What is an immediate change that can be made? What long-term policy and practice adjustments can be put into place?

A. I've been a school board member for a long time, and I often get calls from parents who have questions about things that are happening at one of our schools. Last night, a very upset kindergarten parent called me. Our older kids are in fourth grade together, so we see each other pretty frequently. She heard that the early childhood team is going to be changing up the curriculum to include more topics that speak directly to identity development, especially around race. This parent is afraid that the teachers are going to "put concepts in the heads of these young kids" and teach them things they are not ready for or "don't even see yet." She loves the school, but she doesn't want the teachers to "burst the beautiful bubble" of the lower school. How should you respond?

B. You are an administrator. Parents of a group of children adopted from Asia wish to hold a community event for Asian Lunar New Year. Some of their ideas include letting children burn incense and parents dressing in costume to represent "Year of the Dog" or "Year of the Monkey" etc. Several teachers of Asian descent have informed you that they find these activities to be culturally offensive—in their cultures, incense is burned only on sacred occasions, for example. How would you handle the situation with a clearly devoted (and white) parent body and still support your Asian faculty members?

C. As department chair, one of your new Teachers of Color comes to you with a dilemma. She is on a team that must share resources and plan curricula together. The teachers must agree to a common set of assignments and topics. However, she is uncomfortable with some of the material, which she feels is at best dated and at worst inappropriate or racist. She has ideas for new materials and resources, but every time she brings them up with the team, she is told to "be patient" and "try doing the things that have always worked." She asks what strategies you can offer to help her navigate these team dynamics in service of a better curriculum.

CHAPTER 8

The Role of White Parents in the Pursuit of Racial Literacy and Equity

We need only talk to white young people to quickly discern that many white parents remain relatively silent on issues of race and talking about whiteness in particular. Though there is a pervasive myth that racism is a generational issue, we speak with and interview enough students around the country to know that this is not the case. We hear and see the racial stress that white students feel at the mere mention of race, especially whiteness. We hear the same anxieties of adults echoed in young people: "What if I say the wrong thing?" "I don't want to sound ignorant or not well spoken on this subject." White students remain ill-equipped to discuss race and racism and to navigate a multiracial society.

A recent study by Sesame Workshop and the University of Chicago (Turner, 2019) found that although parents say they are comfortable talking about issues of race, the majority of white parents are rarely, if ever, having conversations with their children about racial topics. Not surprisingly, Parents of Color are more likely to discuss race with their children. Yet, even when white parents do talk about racial identity, many wait until their children are 10 years old or older. So, if parents are not teaching their children about race in a thoughtful manner, our larger culture is more than ready to fill in the gaps in ways that are not helpful. As a result, children end up seeing difference as some kind of deficit and are left to make up their own explanation for what they see. More troubling, most parents talk about racial identity only if their children have heard something negative about their own identity. This partly explains why more Parents of Color are having these conversations with their children. White parents can avoid racial topics because their children are far less likely to come under threat because of their race.

Unfortunately, it is not surprising that white parents are reluctant to speak with their kids about race. Aside from not recognizing the necessity for these discussions, many of us have been raised to believe that to notice race, let alone mention it, is racist, and for decades we have been told that children do not notice race unless someone points it out. We know this is simply untrue. There have been several studies that suggest that babies as young as three to six months old notice skin tone differences, as marked by the amount of time a baby's eyes linger on a person with a different skin tone than their primary caregivers (Kelly et al., 2005). This is not racial prejudice, but it is racial recognition. In a recent study of preschoolers, researchers asked white parents, who did not show any overt racial bias, how biased they believed their white children to be. Most believed their children did not harbor racial prejudice. Yet, many of the children said they would not want Black friends (Moyer, 2020). By five years old, children recognize that different groups are treated differently, and by age ten, children have internalized stereotypes (Steele, 2011). It is never too early to start talking about race.

So how do we prevent raising the next generation of white people who are uncomfortable and avoid talking about race? The only way that can happen is if white adults are able to withstand their own discomfort and intentionally talk about their own racial identity with white kids. A lack of racial awareness prevents us from being able to identify and analyze the many pervasive myths and stereotypes about race, from seeing the structures that give unearned advantage to white people and systematically create obstacles for People of Color. Systems that reinforce inequity are taken for granted, are deeply embedded in our institutions, and often are believed to operate as meritocracies. This is a delusional understanding of the world, and through inaction, we have passed on and modeled these beliefs for our children. In the absence of explicit and direct instruction about race and racism, white children tend to develop a confused and negative view about racial matters. It is also true that if we don't start early with white children, we are setting them up for the overwhelming guilt we so often see in adults.

We know that many white parents want to do something different from the way they were raised. We continuously hear from white parents, often identifying as liberal, about their desire to "do better" and to be more open to conversations about race with their white children. Often in this discussion, however, a competing sentiment is also expressed: the fear that discussions about race will cause their child to feel shame about their race and feel blamed for racism. We suspect that this fear reflects how the parent feels about their own whiteness and privilege, and therefore, the fear of passing those feelings onto their children is absolutely warranted. Just as white teachers must know and understand their own racial identity in order to guide white students, so too must parents cultivate their racial awareness in order to shepherd their children toward racial literacy and antiracism.

We need to acknowledge and address these feelings of white guilt so that we can move on. Ultimately, white guilt is not a position we want to get stuck in because it is a self-focused viewpoint that does nothing to end racial injustice. Again, having a positive white racial identity means understanding the way whiteness shapes our position and experience. And once children understand that racism is not about good and bad people, but about systems and privilege, they can take responsibility, be on the lookout for it, and feel some agency to change it. Children can hold this complexity, and too often our attempts to shield them end up backfiring. Ironically, it is talking to our children about race that will enable them *not* to feel guilty. As one middle school student told us, "Adults think we can't handle the truth, but then how are we supposed to handle it when we find out?"

When white parents believe they *are* talking about race with their children, it is often in generalized terms. Research cited in Po Bronson and Ashley Merryman's *NurtureShock* (2009) reveals how hard it is for white families to talk about being white and what that means for both them and society. They surveyed children whose parents admitted that they did not talk about race. When those children were asked if their parents liked Black people, over 52% of the kids replied with "no" or

"I don't know." Even when not talking explicitly about race, we are still sending messages to our children. We are supporting the status quo and creating a vacuum that leaves our kids vulnerable and susceptible to false information.

Similarly, when parents encourage their kids to "respect everyone" and tell them, "We love all people," children are unable to connect the abstract notion of "respect everyone" to a clear sense of how to be authentic in racial interactions. Bronson and Merryman's research also suggests that general comments about "liking everyone" do not translate into children believing it is true. Even when given messages of equality, offered books with racially diverse characters, and given toys and dolls that represent different racial identities, unless white children saw People of Color in their homes, and saw their parents interact with People of Color, the children still assumed the racial superiority of white people. Children can spot the discrepancies: if everyone is equal, why don't we all live in the same neighborhood or all go to school together? The racial isolation that many white families live in belies any broad statements of a belief in racial equality.

As children get older, not only are they more likely to internalize stereotypes in the absence of discussion, but they can become targets for recruitment by white nationalist groups. In their blog *Inoculating Our Students Against White Nationalism*, Christine Saxman and Shelly Tochluk (2020) warn:

> *Over the past four years, white nationalism has been on the rise inside and outside of schools. White nationalists use the internet like a hunting ground to strategically target young white people. Using YouTube, Instagram, and other online platforms, white nationalists take advantage of algorithms to lure viewers deeper and deeper into their networks and ideology.* (para. 1)

There have been numerous articles recounting the parent's shock upon discovering that their child had been successfully recruited, and the antidote in every case has been to stay in conversation with the child.

Understanding that we never truly arrive at some enlightened state and that it takes sustained effort to disrupt racism, we must also accept that talking about race with our kids must be ongoing and continuous. No matter the age of the child, there are consequences for not discussing race with our children and huge gains when we do. We are all constantly being bombarded with racial myths, stereotypes, and straight up lies. As parents, we need to have enough racial awareness ourselves to make the racially implicit, explicit for our children. The more times we point out the false narratives with our children, the more habitual it becomes for our kids, giving them the tools they need to decode racial untruths they encounter when they are not with us. We can inoculate them, to some degree, from supporting and perpetuating racism.

One of the most powerful ways we can model a healthy racial identity is to tell our kids about the ways we were socialized as white. While they may not seem to be paying attention, they are absorbing our stories and comparing them to the ways they are seeing race operate. Some parents worry about sharing incidents that may be more negative or hurtful, but those can be important stories about resilience. This doesn't mean we need to have all the answers or to be right all the time. We are our child's first model for these kinds of conversations, and simply sharing what it was like for us to grow up can be a first step in countering white silence. Discussing stereotypes that we have acted upon, we can model the importance of interrogating our beliefs and biases and invite dialogue with our kids. Here is an example of a conversation a white mother had with her children when they were in the late elementary years, about 8 and 10 years old.

After watching a television show, she said: "It seems like there are only white girls in that dance class. There were only white people in my ballet class growing up, too, and I just thought it was normal. But later I discovered that some of my Black friends went to a different dance class. I thought, 'Of course! Not only white people like to dance.' So why weren't there any People of Color in my class?"

They went on to have discussions about how People of Color were not allowed in most ballet companies in the past and are often still excluded now. They discussed the myth that only certain bodies would be good at ballet. They discussed standards of beauty and poise and who created those beliefs. They did not have this conversation all at once, but it was one they revisited over time. The conversation then splintered off into looking at racial dynamics within other art forms. Later they went to see Alvin Ailey, a Black-founded modern dance company that features mostly Black dancers, and other concerts and exhibits by Artists of Color. The conversations were not perfect, and she was not always able to answer all their questions, but they were part of an ongoing conversation and inquiry as a family.

Being a single parent and having little extra time, if I (Jenna) read the above scenario, it would have felt entirely aspirational and out of my grasp. However, I was able to bring up race and whiteness enough that my kids later took it upon themselves to understand the reality they saw every day at school. I remember my daughter coming home her freshman year, noting that the school's resource officers were only ever called to "handle" a Student of Color.

Here are a few strategies to consider when talking to your children about race:

- Keep the length of the conversation to the amount of time they are interested. Young people routinely request that racial conversations happen in small doses and with greater frequency rather than having "a big talk." When we follow the lead of children, they usually let us know when they have had enough and if we are talking beyond their developmental capacity.
- Name race, specifically whiteness. Avoid the default of "white, unless stated otherwise." We need not only to normalize conversations about race, but also to make sure "white" is understood as a racial identity. Offer different models of whiteness, including how our race intersects with other identities like gender identity, religion, ability, and social class.
- Make sure your kids understand People of Color are not a monolith. It is important to make explicit the humanity and dignity of all People of Color and to be especially aware to engage in ways that do not describe People of Color only as oppressed and as victims. We do not need children to feel pity nor support a belief in white superiority and the need for white saviors. Children can understand how People of Color have different ethnic

backgrounds and have worked together across differences to challenge racism.

- Name difference as difference and not as deficit. Think of ways to normalize what is not common or known in your household. For example, "I know we all have straight hair in our family, but there are so many types of hair textures and colors." Our kids are always watching us and our reactions when we encounter something new. We can also draw attention to conversations we can avoid as a white family: "I don't have to worry about you getting your driver's license and having a dangerous traffic stop with the police. But if you are ever driving with a friend who is not white, be mindful that the police may not see them the same way they see you."

- Be explicit. If you want to deliver a message akin to "everyone is equal," think about what it is you want to communicate *specifically*. Being "kind or "nice" is not the same as being antiracist: you don't have to respect someone to be kind to them.

- Point out and challenge stereotypes and assumptions. There are plenty of opportunities to do this with books, TV, and other media. It can also be powerful to name assumptions we have or stereotypes that we catch ourselves falling back on. This models that it is common to absorb stereotypes and that there is a need to interrupt them.

- Affirm questions about race. Though it can sometimes feel embarrassing when a child asks a question in public, it is important to welcome curiosity. And it's a moment to think about where your embarrassment is coming from—why are you so uncomfortable? What are you afraid will happen? Modeling curiosity can be a great way to learn something new together.

- Practice activism and advocacy as a family. Giving children opportunities to have a sense of agency and engaging in activism decreases feelings of guilt and overwhelm. Again, it is important that this is not done out of a sense of saving anyone and should be done in solidarity with People of Color whenever possible.

- Finally, desegregate your life. That does not mean to go out and try to acquire Friends of Color, but be more intentional about racial diversity in your own space. Put yourself in places you do not typically go like shopping in grocery stores and trying out restaurants in different neighborhoods.

It is important to know that you are not alone. In addition to being advocates of affinity groups for teachers and students, we are also champions of white antiracist affinity groups for parents. These groups can help shift school culture when they are supporting racial equity initiatives instead of calling them into question or derailing their efforts. Here are some comments made by parents about how an affinity group they attended, facilitated by our colleague Lori Cohen in the Mid-Atlantic area, impacted them and their families.

- I look at the world differently now. I was always aware of a level of privilege I enjoyed, but I have a clearer understanding of it now.
- I can see the roots and structure of systemic racism more clearly now, and I see how nothing will change unless there is structural and systemic change.
- I have been increasingly more comfortable initiating conversations about racism with the people within my sphere of influence and have felt better equipped to do so carefully and with listening ears, based on the readings and group discussions.
- With pretty much every school communication, I'm questioning the equity and thinking about possible ways to improve structures.
- Since starting this work together, I now cannot unsee systemic racism. It is everywhere and in seemingly every facet of American society. I may have understood this at some level before this work, but now it is the lens through which I view almost everything.
- Notions of privilege and white supremacy are common topics in my household since beginning this work.
- I valued the reflection prompts to examine how white supremacy benefits me and my family, which has led to conversations at home that notice and name white supremacy. We have used this to challenge our thinking, name our privilege, and establish a lifelong commitment to learning and supporting antiracist

values and behaviors in our family and community, including at school.

- We have committed, as a family, to participate in all school and district organized or recommended antiracism, Black Lives Matter, Black History Month and year-round school activities to grow our learning.

There are also plenty of amazing resources that can help you get ideas and inspiration to have these conversations with your white children. Here are a few that we use frequently:

Jennifer Harvey. (2017). *Raising white kids: Bringing up children in a racially unjust America*. Abingdon Press.

Ali Michael and Eleonora Bartoli. (2014). *What white children need to know about race*. Independent School.

Melinda Wenner Moyer. (2014, March 30). *Teaching tolerance: How white parents should talk to their young kids about race*. Slate. https://slate.com/human-interest/2014/03/teaching -tolerance-how-white-parents-should-talk-to-their-kids-about -race.html

Raising Race Conscious Children. (2016). 100 race conscious things you can say to your child to advance racial justice. *Raising Race Conscious Children*. http://www.raceconscious .org/2016/06/100-race-conscious-things-to-say-to-your-child-to -advance-racial-justice/

Dana Williams. (2010). *Beyond the golden rule: A parent's guide to preventing and responding to prejudice*. Teaching Tolerance.

White Parents Raising Children Who Identify as People of Color

Given the fact that multiracial children are the fastest growing racial group in the country's schools right now, we want to include the role of racial identity development for white parents/caregivers raising children who identify as both white and People of Color. It's very important that these children embrace all parts of their racial backgrounds and not be forced to choose one identity over the other. They get to be their full selves and embrace the spectrum of their racialized cultures and experiences. This also means they have a *different* racial identity from their monoracial parents even if they share some aspects of whiteness. Many multiracial children have described to us how their awareness of their identity can change given which parent they are with as well as due to larger societal reactions to who they are perceived to be racially, often via the inappropriate question, "So, what are you?"

Therefore, white parents need to double their efforts to explore their own identity development. They need to be firmly rooted in their own understanding of their whiteness so they can support their child's development in healthy ways. Often, multiracial families take the color-aversive approach we described in the first part of the book, pretending that "race doesn't matter" because we are multiracial. There can be the illusion that somehow these families have escaped or transcended racism, but white supremacy can still operate in multiracial households. Additionally, White parents must be careful not to isolate multiracial children from their Communities of Color. They must be sure that their family stays connected with all aspects of their child's ethnic identity.

Another pitfall is when white parents assume they can understand what it means to be a Person of Color just because they are raising a multiracial child. While we can observe, listen, empathize, and support their development, it is not ours. A multiracial experience is filled with nuance and complexity that we don't experience, and that's okay. There are millions of parents raising children who do not share some aspect of their identity. For example, if my child has a learning disability, I may watch the struggle and effort they put forth to navigate school and all the roadblocks thrown in their way. I may support and advocate, attending IEP meetings and teacher conferences. But that doesn't mean I know what it's like to move through the world with my child's particular experience. I am most effective when I think about what school was like for me and all the things I didn't have to deal with, how the path was clear and straight for me. It is then that I can reflect and contextualize my child's experience as different, not comparable. Then I can listen with greater attention and work to make sure I know what they need to be successful, which is very different from what I needed. We encourage all white parents to take a deep dive into their identity and see it as a critical first step to being able to raise children who will have an authentic and developed sense of their own race and how it impacts how they experience and navigate their particular context.

The Impact of White Parents on Racial Equity in Schools

Every parent wants what is best for their child. But what if getting "the best" for your child means making things worse for someone else's? It may just seem like your individual request if you don't realize that hundreds of other white parents may be doing the exact same thing. We must consider the collective impact white parents have on education.

Using my hometown of Charlottesville, Virginia, as an example, I (Jenna) will show some of the ways that white parents have undermined racial equity initiatives within the public schools in the name of doing what is best for their child.

As I mentioned before, in 1958, when the city of Charlottesville was required to desegregate the schools, the governor ordered the city to shut them down rather than integrate. Many white families opted for private schools, and they were able to secure public funding through vouchers, which created a resource vacuum for the public schools when they were forced to reopen a year later (Museum of History and Culture, 2021).

Twenty years later, in response to the demands of white families, the district created a gifted and talented program called Quest, which unsurprisingly, enrolled almost exclusively white children. (Baars, 2019). My sister was chosen to be part of Quest, but I was one of the only white kids who was not in the program. Students selected to be part of Quest were pulled out of regular classrooms and given academic enrichment, such as supplemental arts education, with a separate teacher in a separate room. I remember asking my first-grade teacher who decides which kids are gifted and talented and being quickly shushed and reminded that I had been kept in at recess the previous day for not turning in my homework.

The school district reinforced segregation in various ways for the next several decades, fueled by the desire to keep white families in the public schools. The district implemented testing requirements solely for Black students who wanted to enroll in predominantly white schools, where the majority of resources were being funneled. Even Black students who lived in the areas whose schools served predominantly white students were required to travel to Black schools.

In 1986, the district pooled all students into two middle schools in an effort to support greater racial and economic equity, and the result was that the number of white students declined by twenty percent over the next ten years. As white enrollment decreased, the Quest program tripled in size. In a 2018 article entitled "'You Are Still Black': Charlottesville's Racial Divide Hinders Students," the *New York Times* reported on the state of Virginia's two different types of high school diplomas: "standard" and "advanced." The article noted that Virginia was then one of at least 14 states with this sort of tiered-diploma approach. It is not difficult to guess the racial makeup of the recipients of those diplomas, which obviously determine how competitive a student will be in college admissions or if they even attend college at all (Green & Waldman, 2018).

What undergirds all of this systemic inequality is the belief that districts, schools, and classrooms can only be "good" if there are white students and families in them. This is how white supremacy remains the foundation of education. It is easy to believe that we parents are only acting in the best interest of our child. However, we must also recognize that when we apply "what is best" to an individual—to our child—as opposed to "what is best" for the whole community, we are ultimately endorsing a system that creates winners and losers. We parents would like to believe that pushing for the best for our child does not mean that less is left for those with the least power and resources. But that is exactly what happens. There needs to be a "less than" for some children to be designated "better than."

The first question that undoubtedly arises is, "Isn't this really about socioeconomics more than race?" State exams show that among low-income families, white students achieve higher scores than Black students in all subject areas, and this same pattern is seen among affluent families. Immigrant students of color who are learning English as a second language also score higher than Black students. It is not about socioeconomics. Perhaps it is easy to brush off the story of Charlottesville because it's located in the Jim Crow South. However, researchers at the Center for Education Policy Analysis (CEPA) out of Stanford, found that one third of the 25 districts with the widest racial achievement disparities are in college towns (Reardon et al., 2019).

Though I was slightly surprised to read this statistic, it aligned with my experience. My children attended the public high school in Cambridge, Massachusetts, and the campus sits between Harvard and MIT, among others. Many parents, including myself, chose to send their kids to the high school in Cambridge for the diversity of students and, specifically, the racial diversity—almost two thirds of the students are Students of Color. The well-regarded honors, advanced placement, and international baccalaureate programs keep white families enrolled, and yet there are very few Kids of Color in those classes. In fact, the lowest level classes, called "college prep" and known by most as CP, have been dubbed by students "Colored People." Just as with Charlottesville's gifted and talented program, tracking in any school is just a different form of racial segregation.

It is white people, specifically liberal and highly educated parents, who insist on tracking despite the vast research that it benefits no one. William Mathis, the managing director for the National Education Policy Center, concludes that, "Tracking has, over decades of extensive research, been repeatedly found to be harmful to those enrolled in lower tracks and to provide no significant advantages for higher-tracked students." Though the proponents of tracking cite the ability to funnel greater resources and support to those who need it most, in practice, this is rarely done. Mathis writes that lower track classes, "tend to have watered down curriculum, less-experienced teachers, lowered expectations, more discipline problems and less-engaging lessons." But Mathis urges that it doesn't have to be this way: "When high-quality, enriched curriculum is provided to all students, the effect is to benefit both high achieving and low-achieving students" (Mathis, 2013).

As we described in Chapter 6, there is a direct correlation between teacher expectation and student achievement. Undergirding the support for tracking is the belief that there is such a thing as innate intelligence. Just underneath the belief in a "trackable" cognitive ability is the belief in a superior intelligence. White dominant culture has been allowed to define intelligence and how to measure it. IQ tests were an extension of the eugenics movement, which was created to legitimize and rationalize inhumane practices by white Europeans, such a slavery and colonialism (Benjamin, 2009). Just as the benefits of tracking have been debunked, the existence of a biological intelligence has long since been disproven. Yet innate intellectual ability remains the implicit philosophy at the foundation of tracking. So why are white parents so invested in upholding something that is proven to be untrue?

In the book *Despite the Best Intentions: How Racial Inequality Thrives in Good Schools,* authors Amanda Lewis and John Diamond (2015) lay out with exquisite clarity the disparity between what white liberal parents say they want, such as racial diversity, and their behavior, such as ensuring tracking continues. I remember a white father whose kids went to the same high school as mine telling me of his frustration, "We wanted our kids to go here because of the diversity, but my daughter doesn't have a single Black friend. It is probably because she is in all honors classes, but there must be other places kids get to know each other." This parent brushed past the lack of racial diversity in honors classes and started to look for other solutions for his daughter to have racially diverse friends, as if the fact of racial segregation in tracking was inescapable.

White parents, whether consciously or unconsciously, are aware that this is not the case, or else they would not fight so vehemently to keep their children in higher level classes. As an educator in *Despite the Best Intentions* put it,

> *Trying to do something about the achievement gap will be "met with opposition from white parents because folks who are benefitting from the gap really don't want the attention to be put on the gap because*

they want their kid to have the perfect education. These parents start planning and optimizing for kids in second grade, like it's a war, preparing for battle." (Lewis & Diamond, 2019, p. 135)

It is easy to think, as I did at one time, that I did not really know that this was happening, yet at some level I knew. White people are not simply the lucky beneficiaries of an unjust system. This deliberately inequitable system comes at the cost of Families of Color. Students who are tracked in lower classes are seen as less competitive in college admissions. Parents of Color who fiercely advocate for their children are often labeled as difficult, unreasonable, or even unstable. Worst of all, as a teacher commented in the article *Getting on the Right Track*, by Michelle Higgins, when students discover they are being placed in a lower level class than one of their classmates, "a little bit of light went out of their eyes" (Higgins, 2019).

Most recently, there has been a wave of white parents demanding that curricula aimed at raising racial awareness, and naming whiteness explicitly, be removed from their child's school. As one parent wrote in a highly publicized letter that condemned his daughter's school and its racial equity efforts, "If the administration was genuinely serious about 'diversity,' it would not insist on the indoctrination of its students, and their families, to a single mindset, most reminiscent of the Chinese Cultural Revolution" (Kennedy, 2021).

But more often, white parents undermine school efforts in more subtle ways. We often hear of white parents asking to have their child moved to a different class because they doubt the expertise and knowledge of Teachers of Color. We know of white parents dedicated to ensuring that weighted grades for GPA remain, awarding higher points to higher level classes because "it's only fair; they are working harder." We have heard of parents successfully rerouting bus routes to avoid Communities of Color under the guise that the route was making their child late to school. We have even heard about a school that had two PTAs because white parents felt they needed a place to talk about their children's needs openly, without fear of being called racist. In her podcast series *Nice White Parents*, Chana Joffe-Walt (2020) poses a haunting question: "How can we have equitable schools if our public institutions only respond to these demands if they happen to align with the interests of white parents?"

In his book *Faces at the Bottom of the Well*, Derrick Bell describes functionalism, which is when an inequitable system remains because it serves those who are most powerful. It seems that we, white parents, are the most powerful. Bell argues that there must be a convergence of interests between white people and People of Color for change to happen. He cites the unanimous ruling in *Brown v. Board of Education* as only happening because of the government's interest in selling democracy abroad (Bell, 1992). Segregation was bad press in the fight against communism and contradictory to America's espoused beliefs.

An equitable educational system *is* that convergence of interests; white parents just need to recognize it. The argument for racial integration should not focus on the benefits to white children. But there is also a myth that it will require a sacrifice on the part of white families when, in fact, all children would benefit. Educational segregation has always been a vicious caste system in this country that intentionally creates barriers for People of Color by distributing resources and opportunities inequitably by race. This is not okay.

The research on the benefits of racially integrated schools is deep and vast. In racially integrated schools, there is a documented reduction in prejudice and belief in stereotypes, and an increase in comfort with people from different backgrounds. But there is also an increase in academic engagement (described as losing track of time when focused on academic work), civic participation (practicing activism), and sense of belonging. Though this latter result, of belonging, may seem counter intuitive, researchers have found that in schools where there was a less pronounced "norm," everyone felt more able to be authentically themselves and, therefore, felt a greater sense of belonging. Additionally, because of student belonging and greater comfort with people from diverse backgrounds, students' sense of physical safety also increased in integrated schools (Piazza, 2021). Positive perception in these three areas of well-being—mental, physical, and social—set the stage for white children to support a racially diverse and equitable society as they grow into adulthood.

We white parents are failing our kids when we keep them in racial isolation. Children see the gap between what we say and what we do, and they are learning to do the same. They see the lack of action as a tacit endorsement of the status quo. White children who remain racially isolated are ill-equipped to navigate an increasingly racially diverse world. They lack skills in holding multiple perspectives, negotiating conflict, tolerating uncertainty, and managing adaptability. What's more, our white children are angry and feel betrayed when they learn that they have not been given the full picture. When confronted with truths about gross racial inequalities, white children often say, "Why didn't anyone ever tell me this?" As Heather McGhee explains in her book *The Sum of Us*, "As with all aspects of racism, the targeted communities bear the brunt—but you don't have to look far to find the collateral damage to the rest of society" (McGhee, 2021).

White parents of school-aged children have an opportunity to make change, and we also have the power to do it. There are loud parent voices opposing accurate history and critical analysis of how race operates in this country. We need louder parent voices demanding it. We can choose to raise the next generation of white people to think and do differently. We can choose to *not* replicate white supremacy culture and racism in our children's schools. When we don't make these choices, we uphold and collude with racism.

There are some organizations that have been created specifically for parents to get involved in antiracist efforts. Integrated Schools is one such organization, whose mission says: "Through outreach, advocacy, and community building, Integrated Schools mobilizes families— particularly those who are white and/or privileged—to practice antiracist school integration" (Integrated Schools, 2021). There are other organizations and models of successful integration efforts, but we need to care enough to change.

We need to step up and follow the leadership from Families of Color who have been the most impacted and organized. We must fund existing efforts and stay engaged when momentum wanes. We need to continue to learn and to challenge the status quo. We need to not feed into the lies that say racial hierarchy benefits someone in the long term. Ultimately, we need to stand in our own integrity as parents and live our values.

CASE STUDIES FOR PARENTS

1. You are on the Parent School Committee. Members of that committee have been preparing a new video they made to show at the annual fundraiser. The video is focused on the extracurricular programming that the school will be able to provide using the money they raise at the event. They want to preview the video with the full committee before the fundraiser. The video ends with a close-up of a young Black girl smiling. One parent says that they will pause on that frame and leave it up during the event because, "her face will help pull on heartstrings." As you hear this, it feels clear that the video is exploiting this girl.

   • How can you bring up this concern?
   • What assumptions and root issues are at the core of your concern?
   • What would you say?

2. Your friend, who has a daughter in the same grade as your daughter, calls to tell you that the classroom assignments have just been released. She is lamenting that while your daughter was assigned to the veteran white teacher, who is adored by all of her students, *her* daughter was put in the class with a new teacher, who she notes is Filipina American. Your friend is clearly distraught and is strategizing about what to do to make sure her daughter has the best possible fourth grade experience. After questioning the new teacher's ability to even teach English, since it is "obviously not her first language," she mentions that she is planning to contact the principal and call in a favor. "After all, we served on the block party committee together last year. I am pretty sure he wants me as a happy parent at the school."

   • What is worrisome about what your friend shared?
   • What assumptions and root issues are at the core of your concern?
   • What would you say?

AFTERWORD

We wrote this book in what undoubtedly has been the toughest year in recent memory for educators. The COVID-19 global pandemic and uprisings around the country protesting racial violence have made teaching, already one of the most difficult jobs, more unreasonable and unsustainable. At the same time, we have seen that education *can* change on a dime when we think it is a life or death matter. Racism is life or death. Movements for racial justice are now starting to face a new round of pushback. As always happens, the pendulum is starting to swing back, as we see states taking up legislation to address what teachers can and cannot say about race in their classrooms. This pattern is not new, but it adds a layer of complexity.

We hear and see the racial anxiety of white people who feel they are under pressure: "If I say it wrong, I will be called racist. If I don't say anything, I'll be called racist," expressing a "damned if we do, damned if we don't" sentiment. We're worried about our relationships with Colleagues of Color and about keeping relationships with other white people. And it's paralyzing because we fear that if we say the wrong thing, it may lead to a "Scarlet R" moment: If I get called a "racist," that's the *end* of the relationship. So, I'm gonna just sit here and be uncomfortable—and silent.

The fear is real. White people will pounce on each other if they make a mistake and can be unforgiving around issues of race. As we described, this is a predictable stage of pseudoindependent behavior: "I know better than you, and I'm going to punish you and show you just how righteous I am. And while I go after *your* racism, I don't have to look at *mine*." We get caught in an endless loop that keeps us from moving forward because judgment will kill any curiosity we have as to why our behavior may be getting in the way.

But the biggest problem is that when we don't do anything, we're still supporting racism.

So, how about we just assume it's us. We are the one making racist comments or acting in ways that support racism. We have to stop pretending racism is someone else's issue and that there's no racism unless someone calls it out. Racism is operating all the time. We do not need more information, another survey, another panel discussion to make sure this is "really an issue." It is. And it is ours.

Let's get busy doing things differently, because if we don't, the harm continues. Beyond this book, there are so many pathways forward. We just need the will and understanding that our students are at stake when we continue to stall, wring our hands, and defend what has always been done. Educators are some of the most caring and creative people of any profession. So much is possible if we work together.

Do we finally want to know, learn, and do better? Or do we want to keep pretending we can continue to avoid and ignore what's really going on? It is time to stop all the worry. No more what ifs. No more hedging our bets. No more letting stuff go unaddressed. No more silence.

APPENDIX A

The Costs of Racism to White People

[Inspired by Paul Kivel's (2011) list in *Uprooting Racism*]

During the opening of their White Privilege Conference, high school students asked all white participants to read through this list and check any items that applied to them. They then read the statements out loud and asked participants to stand if the statement was true for them.

1. ____ I often feel or observe social awkwardness between People of Color and white people.
2. ____ I miscommunicate with People of Color.
3. ____ I can miss or avoid meeting People of Color who could expand my perspective or be my friends.
4. ____ I feel a pressure to withhold myself and not put myself out there for fear of offending a Person of Color or for being perceived as racist.
5. ____ People of Color don't trust me because I'm white.
6. ____ I can be perceived as racist if I'm white no matter what I do. So, I'm guilty until proven innocent.
7. ____ I have felt an emotional toll on me as I watch Friends of Color deal with racism, yet I can't share their experience. This creates emotional distance between me and my friends and people I love.

8. _____ White culture is seen as "Wonder Bread," empty, boring compared to other racial groups.

9. _____ I have felt embarrassed by, separate from, superior to, or more tolerant than other white people.

10. _____ I have felt frustrated, angry, tired, or weary about dealing with racism and hearing about racial affairs.

11. _____ I grew up, lived, live in a neighborhood, or go to a school or camp that was or is almost exclusively white.

12. _____ I am unaware of my ethnic background because my family changed its name when it came to this country to fit in and assimilate.

13. _____ I am not in a close, significant relationship with any People of Color in my life right now.

14. _____ I have participated in an organization, group, event, or meeting that People of Color protested as racist, or that I knew to be racist, and did nothing about it.

15. _____ I have been nervous and fearful or found myself stiffening up when encountering People of Color in a neutral public space, such as on the street, in an elevator, etc.

16. _____ I have felt that people of other racial groups were more spiritual than white people.

17. _____ I have heard degrading jokes, comments, or put-downs about People of Color made in my presence and did not protest or challenge them.

18. _____ I was in a close friendship or relationship with a Person of Color where the relationship was affected, stressed, or endangered by racism between us or from others.

19. _____ I have felt racial tension or noticed racism in a situation and was afraid to say or do anything about it.

20. _____ I live in a community where, for whatever reason, no People of Color are present, so some of these questions don't apply.

APPENDIX B

White Antiracist Activists

Compiled by Elizabeth Denevi and Lori Cohen,
Eastern Educational Resource Collaborative

What We Mean by "White Antiracist Activist"

Antiracism for white people is a process of recognizing the impact of race as a system of oppression and of engaging in practices, behaviors, and ways of being that disrupt racial discrimination. Racism advantages white people and disadvantages People of Color via inequitable systems of institutional power, authority, and violence. The term "People of Color" includes Native, Black/African American, Latinx, Asian American/Pacific Islander, Middle Eastern, and Multiracial People. More accurately, this group is referred to as "people of the global majority." The goal of this activism is to challenge the racist status quo in order to bring about social change, healing, and liberation for non-white-identified communities. The following people and organizations are white antiracist/antioppression activists who questioned, resisted, and interrupted racist systems.

People of Color have always worked to end racism. By naming these white activists and organizations, we hope to show that for as long as there has been racial oppression, particularly in the United States, there have been white people who have stood in solidarity with People of Color. By highlighting these white activists, we hope to expand the understanding of how white people can work toward racial justice in proactive and productive ways. Much of what our students learn in schools about race reflects People of Color as oppressed and white people as bad racists, but the realities of antioppression/antiracism work are far more nuanced and complex.

To disrupt the narratives we learned in schools, and to support white students in recognizing their empowerment in antiracist work, we share a collection of noted white antiracist/antioppression activists whose work can serve as a guidepost. We also recognize that these activists are products of their particular times and reflect the limitations of their time periods. We also offer these examples as a way for white educators to think about their personal stake and role in challenging racism in their classrooms. This list is by no means exhaustive, but for those looking to build a curriculum, we hope you will find this list a helpful starting point. This is an attempt to highlight the work of white activists who stood up to racism when it was challenging, unpopular, and even illegal.

As a means of studying and learning from these activists, we offer these critical questions for consideration:

1. In considering the activists' lives, what were the significant moments that led to their activism? What motivated them to work for change?
2. What skills do/did they need to challenge racial injustice?
3. What unconscious or hidden bias/perspectives might these activists have?
4. How can white people work effectively in solidarity with People of Color? How can they keep from replicating the very system they are trying to challenge?
5. What is the value of a multiracial, antiracist coalition?
6. What actions might you take to work for racial justice?

The African Free School was founded by members of the New York Manumission Society in 1794 to provide education to children of enslaved and free People of Color. Many of the school's students became leaders in the African American community in New York. The first school was a one-room schoolhouse that held about 40 students. Originally the Manumission Society hired white teachers, but it eventually employed Black teachers as well. By 1835, when the schools ended their run as privately supported institutions and were integrated into the public school system, the African Free School had seven buildings in different neighborhoods and had educated thousands of children. This was several years after New York freed the last adult slaves under its gradual abolition law.

Anne McCarty Braden (1924–2006) was a journalist and community organizer from Louisville, Kentucky, who defied racist real estate practices and the House Un-American Activities Committee and organized white Southerners to support the civil rights movement. She is best known for helping a Black couple buy a house in an all-white neighborhood of Louisville, Kentucky, in 1954. She and her husband were put on trial for sedition, banned from jobs, threatened, and reviled by their fellow white Southerners for what they did. She wrote a book about her sedition trial, *The Wall Between*, which was nominated for the National Book Award. She worked closely with Rosa Parks and Ella Baker, and she is mentioned in Dr. King's *Letter from a Birmingham Jail*.

John Brown (1800–1859) was also an ardent abolitionist who worked with the Underground Railroad and worked to inspire a slave insurrection at Harpers Ferry, West Virginia. As a 12-year-old boy traveling through Michigan, Brown witnessed an enslaved African American boy being beaten, which haunted him for years and informed his own abolitionism. In 1855, Brown moved to Kansas, and with the passing of the Kansas–Nebraska Act of 1854, there was conflict over whether the territory would be a free or a slave state. Brown, who believed in using violent means to end slavery, became involved in the conflict; in 1856, he and several of his men killed five pro-slavery settlers in a retaliatory attack at Pottawatomie Creek. With the intent of inspiring a slave insurrection, he eventually led an unsuccessful raid on the Harpers Ferry federal armory on October 16, 1859, holding dozens of men hostage. Brown's forces held out for two days; they were eventually defeated by military forces led by Robert E. Lee. Many of Brown's men were killed, including two of his sons, and he was captured. Brown went to trial and was executed on December 2, 1859.

Edgar Chandler (1904–1988) was a Navy Chaplain, congregational minister, and director of the Church Federation of Greater Chicago during the 1960s, and he worked closely with Martin Luther King Jr. Chandler later hired Jesse Jackson at the Church Federation of Greater Chicago and they became friends. Jackson was quoted as saying, Chandler "really helped to bring me into the civil rights movement. . . He helped to hire me when I had no money and helped sustain my family."

Christopher Chandler (1938–2019) was a longtime journalist who focused on social justice issues, helped start the Chicago Journalism Review, the Chicago Free Press, and the Daily Planet, and worked on exposés of the 1969 police raid that resulted in the killings of Black Panther leaders Fred Hampton and Mark Clark. Later, he was Press Secretary for Chicago Mayor Harold Washington, and later for US Representative Bobby Rush. From 1997 to 2001, Chandler worked in media relations for the Government Accountability Project, a Washington, DC, group that assists whistleblowers.

Prudence Crandall (1803–1890) was an American schoolteacher and activist. She is believed to have run the first known school for Black girls in the United States: When Crandall admitted Sarah Harris, a 20-year-old African American female student, to her school in 1832, Crandall had what is considered to be the first integrated classroom in the United States. Parents of the white children began to withdraw them. She decided that if white girls would not attend, she would educate Black girls. She was arrested and spent a night in jail. Soon the violence of the townspeople forced her to close the school and leave.

Virginia Foster Durr (1903–1999) was a housewife and political activist from Birmingham, Alabama, who fought against the poll tax and Southern white male domination. Durr was a close friend of Rosa Parks and Eleanor Roosevelt and was the sister-in-law (through her sister's marriage) of Supreme Court Justice Hugo Black, who sat on many crucial civil rights cases. In 1933, Durr moved with her husband to Washington, DC, which was where her activism began. She met important people through her husband's New Deal contacts, some of whom changed her conservative views on civil matters. Durr joined the Woman's National Democratic Club, and in 1938, she was one of the founding members of the Southern Conference for Human Welfare, an interracial group working to reduce segregation and improve living conditions in the South. The group was formed, in part, as a response to Franklin Roosevelt's proclamation that the South was the leading economic problem in the nation. By 1941, Durr became the vice president of the Southern Conference for Human Welfare's civil rights subcommittee. Working together with First Lady Eleanor Roosevelt, she lobbied for legislation to abolish the poll tax. She worked jointly with liberal political leaders to gain the necessary support needed for legislation, which ultimately resulted in the passing of the Voting Rights Act of 1965.

Jane Elliott (1933–), in response to the assassination of Martin Luther King Jr. in 1968, devised the controversial and startling "Blue Eyes/ Brown Eyes" exercise. This exercise labels participants as inferior or superior based solely on the color of their eyes and exposes them to the experience of being a minority. Elliott's classroom exercise was filmed the third time she held it with her white third graders in 1970, becoming the documentary *The Eye of the Storm*. This in turn inspired a retrospective that reunited the 1970 class members with their teacher fifteen years later in "A Class Divided," an episode of the PBS series *Frontline*. After leaving her school, Elliott became a full-time diversity educator. She still holds the exercise and gives lectures about its effects all over the United States.

Bob Fletcher (1911–2013) was a farmer, fireman, and community historian best known for safeguarding the farms of expelled Japanese Americans in Florin, California, during World War II. With the attack on Pearl Harbor and the eviction of West Coast Japanese Americans looming, the Tsukamoto family of Florin approached Fletcher with a proposal: would he manage the Flame Tokay grape farms of two of their friends, paying taxes and mortgages, while they were excluded? Fletcher agreed, quit his job, and eventually took over the farms of the Okamoto, Nitta, and Tsukamoto families, a total of ninety acres. In doing so, he bucked popular opinion that largely supported the exclusion of Japanese Americans and opposed their return. He was, in fact, shot at while in the Tsukamotos' barn. When the families returned from their incarceration in the fall of 1945, their farms and homes were intact, and their half of the profits was waiting for them. Fletcher continued to help the families after the war, sometimes buying supplies and equipment for them when local businesses would not sell to them. In the later part of the twentieth century, with changing attitudes toward the wartime incarceration, Fletcher received acclaim for his wartime actions. He died at the age of 101, his actions celebrated in obituaries in the *New York Times* and other newspapers.

William Lloyd Garrison (1805–1879) was a prominent American abolitionist, journalist, suffragist, and social reformer. He is best known for his widely read antislavery newspaper *The Liberator*, which he founded in 1831 and published in Boston until slavery in the United States was abolished by Constitutional amendment in 1865. He was one of the founders of the American Anti-Slavery Society, and he promoted immediate and uncompensated, as opposed to gradual and compensated, emancipation of slaves in the United States. Garrison also emerged as a leading advocate of women's rights, which prompted a split in the abolitionist community. In the 1870s, Garrison became a prominent voice for the women's suffrage movement.

Andrew Goodman (1943–1964) and **Michael Henry "Mickey" Schwerner** (1939–1964) were American civil rights activists who were murdered at a young age by members of the Ku Klux Klan. They took part in the Freedom Summer campaign to register African Americans to vote in Mississippi, where they met fellow social activist James Chaney. They all worked together in Meridian, Mississippi, where Schwerner was designated head of the field office. The Mississippi State Sovereignty Commission was strongly opposed to integration and civil rights and paid spies to identify citizens suspected of activism, especially people from the North and West who entered the state. On their return to Meridian, the three men were stopped and arrested by Deputy Sheriff Cecil Price (a Klan member) for allegedly driving 35 miles per hour over the 30-mile-per-hour speed limit. They were arrested, released, and eventually turned over to Klansmen who shot and killed them. The Commission was eventually implicated in the murders of Chaney, Goodman, and Schwerner.

Sarah Moore Grimké (1792–1873) and **Angelina Emily Grimké** (1805–1879), known as the Grimké sisters, were speakers, writers, and educators who were the first nationally known white American female advocates for women's rights and the abolition of slavery. They grew up in a slave-owning family in South Carolina but moved to the North in the 1820s, settling for some time in Philadelphia and becoming part of its substantial Quaker community. They became deeply involved with the abolitionist movement, traveling on its lecture circuit and recounting their firsthand experiences with slavery on their family's plantation. Among the first white American women to act publicly in social reform movements, they were ridiculed for their abolitionist activity and perspective. They also became early activists in the women's rights movement.

Rachelle Horowitz was an organizer and strategist during the height of the modern civil rights movement and is a major figure in labor union politics. As a student member of the socialist party during the late 1950s, Horowitz was encouraged to become involved in the civil rights movement by party leaders who recognized the leadership potential that she and other young members possessed. She worked with organizer Bayard Rustin on the March on Washington in 1963, assisting with planning for demonstrations and labor organization efforts and securing transportation to get leaders, organizations, and march participants to and from Washington, DC. Horowitz also assisted Rustin with running the march's organizing headquarters in New York. In the following year, Horowitz spent three months in Jackson, Mississippi, for the formation of the Freedom Democrats, and she assisted with organizing Freedom Summer. She also continued to work with Rustin, serving as his assistant from 1964 to 1973, and worked with him and others to form the Social Democrats. She continued her efforts with labor unions throughout the 1970s and served as the political director of the American Federation of Teachers from 1974 to 1995.

William Loren Katz (1927–2019) was an American educator, activist, historian, and author of 40 books on African American history, including a number of titles for young adult readers. He was particularly noted for his research and writing on the 500-year history of relations between African Americans and Native Americans. His books include *Breaking the Chains: African American Slave Resistance, The Black West,* and *Black Women of the Old West.* Katz taught in New York City and the state's public secondary education systems for 14 years. He served as a consultant to the US Senate; the British House of Commons; the Smithsonian Institution; the state boards of education of North Carolina and New York; and school districts from California to Florida and England. His lifetime commitment to narrating an inclusive and truthful American history and to combating fascism and racism affirms the power of populist historiography and of publishing.

Eric Kulberg was a photographer at the March on Washington in 1963. Only 18 years old at the time, Kulberg convinced his supervisors that he needed to be at the march to document the experience. After some initial resistance, his bosses relented and supported Kulberg's decision. One of the only photographers to capture the experience in color film, Kulberg generated some of the most iconic images of the experience. He also was changed by what he witnessed. Standing mere feet from Dr. Martin Luther King Jr. as he spoke, Kulberg had two revelations: he wanted to eradicate prejudice, and he wanted to center the experience of African Americans through radio, film, and television—which is how Kulberg spent most of his career.

Margaret Leonard was a Freedom Rider and civil rights activist. When she was a student at Sophie Newcomb College in New Orleans, Louisiana, she began going to Congress of Racial Equality meetings and participated in both local sit-ins and the Freedom Rides of 1961. At Congress of Racial Equality meetings, she learned about the practices of nonviolent resistance that became the mainstay of the Freedom Riders movement. She was the first unmistakably Southern white student to participate in the Mississippi Freedom Ride, and she inspired other white people to follow her lead. Leonard is now retired from a reporting career at the *St. Petersburg Times*, *Miami Herald*, and *Tallahassee Democrat* and still occasionally unites with other Freedom Riders.

Viola Liuzzo (1925–1965) was a Unitarian Universalist civil rights activist from Michigan. In March 1965, Liuzzo, then a housewife and mother of five with a history of local activism, heeded the call of Martin Luther King Jr. and traveled from Detroit, Michigan, to Selma, Alabama, in the wake of the Bloody Sunday attempt at marching across the Edmund Pettus Bridge. Liuzzo participated in the successful Selma to Montgomery marches and helped with coordination and logistics. Driving back from a trip shuttling fellow activists to the Montgomery airport, she was shot dead by members of the Ku Klux Klan at age 39.

Richard Loving (1933–1975) was married to Mildred Loving, and they were plaintiffs in the landmark US Supreme Court case *Loving v. Virginia* (1967). The Lovings were an interracial married couple who were criminally charged under a Virginia statute banning such marriages. With the help of the American Civil Liberties Union (ACLU), they filed suit to overturn the law. In 1967, the Supreme Court ruled in their favor, striking down the Virginia statute and all state antimiscegenation laws as unconstitutional violations of the Fourteenth Amendment.

Hazel Massey (born Hazel Bryan 1941–) first appeared in an iconic photograph in 1957, as she leered at the Little Rock Nine, nine Black students who were integrated at Central High School. Bryan is captured shouting at Elizabeth Eckford, who is also featured in this photograph. Bryan, only 17 years old at the time and a high school dropout, was haunted by the image for which she became notorious. Several years after the photograph was taken, Bryan tracked Eckford down and apologized. The two women forged a friendship for a number of years, and in 1999, journalist David Margolick decided to write *Elizabeth and Hazel*, two years after the 40th anniversary of the events in Little Rock.

William Lewis Moore (1927–1963) was a postal worker and Congress of Racial Equality member who staged lone protests against racial segregation. Moore undertook three civil rights protests in which he marched to a capital to hand-deliver letters he had written denouncing racial segregation. Moore set out on a one-man civil rights march to Jackson, Mississippi, to implore Mississippi Governor Ross Barnett to support integration efforts. He wore signs that stated: "End Segregation in America, Eat at Joe's—Both Black and white" and "Equal Rights for All (Mississippi or Bust)." On April 23, 1963, Moore was found dead on US Highway 11 near Attalla, Alabama—four days shy of his 36th birthday. A letter he had written, meant for Governor Ross, was opened when Moore was found, and its contents stated that "the white man cannot be truly free himself until all men have their rights."

Joan Trumpauer Mulholland, a white teenager in the South during Segregation, put herself on the front lines of the civil rights struggle. *She Stood for Freedom* is a biography about her experiences, published simultaneously in picture book and middle-grade editions, that details the many events she participated in. She attended demonstrations and sit-ins and was one of the 1961 Freedom Riders who was arrested and put on death row at the notorious Parchman Penitentiary for months. She was the first White person to join in the 1963 Woolworth's lunch counter sit-ins in Jackson, Mississippi, and that same year she participated in the March on Washington with Dr. Martin Luther King Jr. She joined the Selma to Montgomery march in 1965, which contributed to the passage of the landmark Voting Rights Act that year. Her willingness to stand up for justice has been an inspiration.

Peter George Norman (1942–2006) was an Australian track athlete who won the silver medal in the 200 meters at the 1968 Summer Olympics in Mexico City. Norman is best known as the third athlete pictured in a famous photograph of the 1968 Olympics Black Power salute, which occurred during the medal ceremony for the 200-meter event. He wore a badge of the Olympic Project for Human Rights in support of fellow athletes John Carlos and Tommie Smith. Norman was not selected for the 1972 Summer Olympics, and he retired from the sport soon after.

Mary White Ovington (1865–1951) was an American suffragist, journalist, and cofounder of the National Association for the Advancement of Colored People (NAACP). Ovington became involved in the campaign for civil rights in 1890 after hearing Frederick Douglass speak in a New York City church. She also supported work to improve living conditions in tenements and investigated housing and employment discrimination.

Theodore Parker (1810–1860) was an American transcendentalist and reforming minister of the Unitarian church. A reformer and abolitionist, his words and popular quotes would later be mentioned in speeches by Abraham Lincoln and Martin Luther King Jr. In Boston, he led the movement to combat the stricter Fugitive Slave Act, a controversial part of the Compromise of 1850. This act required law enforcement and citizens of all states—free states as well as slave states—to assist in recovering fugitive slaves. He and his followers formed the Boston Vigilance Committee, which refused to assist with the recovery of fugitive slaves and which helped to hide them. For example, they smuggled away Ellen and William Craft when Georgian slave catchers came to Boston to arrest them. Due to such efforts, between 1850 and the onset of the American Civil War in 1861, slaves were captured in Boston and transported back to the South only twice.

Joachim Prinz (1902–1998) devoted much of his life in the United States to the civil rights movement. He saw the plight of African Americans in the context of his own experience under Hitler. From his early days as a rabbi in Newark, he spoke from his pulpit about the disgrace of discrimination. He joined the picket lines across America, protesting racial prejudices from unequal employment to segregated schools, housing, and all other areas of life. While serving as president of the American Jewish Congress, he represented the Jewish community as an organizer of the August 1963 March on Washington. He came to the podium immediately following a stirring spiritual, sung by the gospel singer Mahalia Jackson, and just before Martin Luther King Jr. delivered his famous "I Have a Dream" speech. Dr. Prinz's address is remembered for its contention that, based on his experience as a rabbi in Nazi Germany after the rise of Hitler, in the face of discrimination, the most immediate and dangerous problem is silence.

Fred Rogers (1928–2003) was an American television personality, musician, puppeteer, writer, producer, and Presbyterian minister. He was the creator, showrunner, and host of the preschool television series *Mister Rogers' Neighborhood*, which ran from 1968 to 2001. While Fred Rogers benefited from a system of advantages for white people, he sought to create a show that could repair some inequities. For example, Francois Clemmons—an African American actor—was an integral part of the show and he depicted a loving, positive role model. Further, the audience for the show was mixed race, indicating that the show appealed to all children. Finally, the documentary *Won't You Be My Neighbor* sought to include significant historical context about race to deepen the movie's message about inclusion and belonging.

Sally Rowley (1931–2020). While working as a secretary in New York in the early 1960s, Rowley joined the Freedom Riders, a group of activists who traveled to the south to challenge segregationist policies. She was arrested in Jackson, Mississippi, in 1961 and served time in the Mississippi State Penitentiary.

Christine Saxman, teacher and racial equity consultant, and **Shelly Tochluk**, professor of education and counselor, have worked together to identify white nationalist groups and their recruiting tactics. They have done intensive research to document how these groups target young people, particularly white boys, and to provide resistance strategies and resources for parents, schools, and young people. See "Inoculating Our Students Against White Nationalism" (https://www .teachingwhilewhite.org/blog/2020/4/13/inoculating-our-students -against-white-nationalism) for an example of their work.

Robert Shetterly is an artist whose series of portraits, *Americans Who Tell the Truth*, has given him an opportunity to speak with children and adults all over the United States about the necessity of dissent in a democracy, the obligations of citizenship, sustainability, US history, and how democracy cannot function if politicians don't tell the truth, if the media don't report it, and if the people don't demand it. Shetterly has engaged in a wide variety of political and humanitarian work with many of the people whose portraits he has painted. In the spring of 2007, he traveled to Rwanda with Lily Yeh and Terry Tempest Williams to work in a village of survivors of the 1994 genocide there. Much of his current work focuses on honoring and working with the activists who are trying to bring an end to the terrible practice of mountaintop removal by coal companies in Appalachia, climate change, and the continuation of systemic racism in the United States, particularly in relation to the school-to-prison pipeline.

Gloria Steinem (1934–) is an American journalist, feminist activist, organizer, and writer. In 2013, she was awarded the Presidential Medal of Freedom by President Barack Obama. With Dorothy Pittman-Hughes, Steinem cofounded *Ms.* magazine and the Women's Action Alliance, a pioneering national information center that specialized in nonsexist, multiracial children's education. The partnership between Steinem and Pitman Hughes began in the early 1970s as the pair took to the podium to discuss the importance of intersectional feminism. She is the founding president of the Ms. Foundation for Women, a national multiracial, multiissue fund that supports grassroots projects to empower women and girls, and also a founder of Take Our Daughters to Work Day, the first national day devoted to girls, which has now become an institution in the United States and in other countries. She was a member of the Beyond Racism Initiative, a three-year effort on the part of activists and experts from South Africa, Brazil, and the United States to compare the racial patterns of those three countries and to learn cross-nationally. She works with the Sophia Smith Collection at Smith College on documenting the grassroots origins of the US women's movement and on a school for organizers in tribute to Wilma Mankiller, Principal Chief of the Cherokee Nation.

Laura Towne (1825–1901) was an American abolitionist and educator. She is best known for forming the first freedmen's schools (those for newly freed slaves), notably the Penn School. She was raised in Philadelphia hearing sermons about the abolition of slavery. Influenced by these teachings, Towne answered the call for volunteers when the Union captured Port Royal and other South Carolina Sea Islands. She and her Quaker friend Ellen Murray founded the Penn Center on St. Helena Island, the first school for newly freed slaves in the United States.

James Tyson partnered with Bree Newsome to remove the Confederate flag that was flying over the South Carolina Statehouse on June 27, 2015. The two 30-year-old Charlotte activists, who had met only a few days before, hustled toward the flagpole bearing the South's most controversial flag. Tyson braced himself so Newsome, strapped into climbing gear, could use his leg to jump the four-foot fence. Tyson, who stood quietly at the base of the pole while Bree climbed, remained in the background. That was the plan, to show white support without dominating. After scaling the flagpole and taking down the flag, Newsome and Tyson were arrested. The state legislature voted to remove the flag permanently less than three weeks later.

Julius Waties Waring (1880–1968) was a US District Judge of the US District Court for the Eastern District of South Carolina who played an important role in the early legal battles of the American civil rights movement and who opened white primaries to Black voters. Waring spent the early part of his career in Charleston, South Carolina, but after political, editorial, and social leaders in South Carolina criticized and shunned Judge Waring and his wife for their progressive views, he and his wife moved to New York City, and he quickly transitioned from a racial moderate to a proponent of radical change. During his career, he fought against racial segregation and worked toward equal opportunities for the Black community in political, economic, and educational spheres.

The Weathermen, also known as the Weather Underground Organization (WUO), was a radical left militant organization active in the late 1960s and 1970s, founded on the Ann Arbor campus of the University of Michigan. The WUO, organized in 1969 as a faction of Students for a Democratic Society (SDS), was largely composed of the national office leadership of SDS and their supporters. Beginning in 1974, the WUO's express political goal was to create a revolutionary party to overthrow what it viewed as American imperialism. In 1969, the WUO authored a position paper, distributed at an SDS convention in Chicago, which called for a white fighting force to be allied with the Black Liberation Movement and other radical movements to destroy US imperialism in favor of a classless communist society. The FBI classified the WUO as a domestic terrorist group with revolutionary positions characterized by Black Power and opposition to the Vietnam War. In the 1970s, the WUO took part in a range of bombing campaigns within the United States and they began to disintegrate after the United States reached a peace accord in Vietnam in 1973. The group was defunct by 1977.

The White Rose (German: *Weiße Rose*) was a nonviolent, intellectual resistance group in Nazi Germany led by a group of students, including Hans and Sophie Scholl. The group conducted an anonymous leaflet and graffiti campaign that called for active opposition to the Nazi regime. Their activities started in Munich in 1942 and ended with the arrest of the core group by the Gestapo in February 1943. They, as well as other members and supporters of the group who carried on distributing the pamphlets, faced show trials by the Nazi People's Court (*Volksgerichtshof*), and many of them were sentenced to death or imprisonment. The group wrote, printed, and initially distributed their pamphlets in the greater Munich region. Later, secret carriers brought copies to other cities, mostly in the southern parts of Germany. In total, the White Rose authored six leaflets, which were multiplied and disbursed—a total of about 15,000 copies. They denounced the Nazi regime's crimes and oppression and called for resistance. In their second leaflet, they openly denounced the persecution and mass murder of the Jews. By the time of their arrest, the members of the White Rose were just about to establish contacts with other German resistance groups like the Kreisau Circle or the Schulze-Boysen/Harnack group of the Red Orchestra. Today, the White Rose is well known both within Germany and worldwide.

Dave Zirin (1974–) is an American political sportswriter. He is the sports editor for *The Nation*, a weekly progressive magazine dedicated to politics and culture; he also writes a blog named *Edge of Sports: The Weekly Sports Column by Dave Zirin* and has authored nine books, including *The John Carlos Story: The Sports Moment That Changed the World*. Zirin has repeatedly called for sports boycotts of certain teams, states, or nations for political reasons, including a boycott against sports teams from Arizona as a statement against the Arizona immigration law. He has criticized Hank Williams Jr. for racist remarks about Barack Obama and has defended baseball player Barry Bonds, noting that most criticisms against Bonds were rooted in racism.

James Zwerg (1939–) is an American former minister who was involved with the Freedom Riders in the early 1960s. He participated in a one-semester student exchange program in 1961 at Fisk University, a predominantly Black school, and met John Lewis, who was a member of the Student Nonviolent Coordinating Committee. As a Freedom Rider, Zwerg traveled by bus to Birmingham, where he was first arrested for not moving to the back of the bus with his Black seating companion, Paul Brooks. Three days later, the Riders regrouped and headed to Montgomery. At first the bus station there was an eerie quiet, but the scene turned into an ambush with the Riders attacked from all directions. Zwerg was denied prompt medical attention because there were no white ambulances available, and he remained unconscious for two days. His post-riot photos were published in many newspapers and magazines across the country.

APPENDIX C

Cycle of Oppression

Source: Adapted from Hardiman & Jackson.

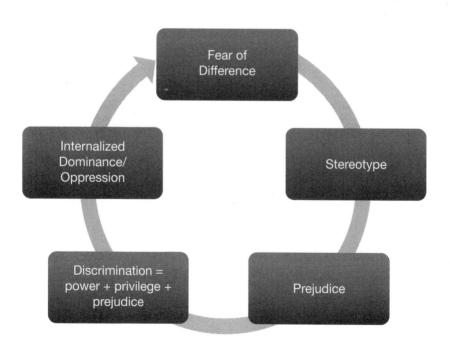

BIBLIOGRAPHY

Accapadi, M. M. (2007). When white women cry: How white women's tears oppress Women of Color. *College Student Affairs Journal, 26*(2), 208–215.

Afeni Mills, A., Chandler-Ward, J., & Denevi, E. (2020, Sept 28). *Evolving our narratives about race in schools*. Teaching While White. https://www.teachingwhilewhite.org/blog/evolving-our-narratives-about-race-in-schools

Annamma, S. A., Jackson, D. D., & Morrison, D. (2017). Conceptualizing color-evasiveness: using dis/ability critical race theory to expand a color-blind racial ideology in education and society. *Race Ethnicity and Education, 20*(2), 147–162.

Baars, S. (May 2, 2019). Quest in Context: Troubled roots of city's gifted program. Cville Weekly. https://www.c-ville.com/quest-in-context/

Baldwin, J. (1972). *No name in the street*. Michael Joseph.

Barnum, M. (2021, July 8). *As states place new limits on class discussions of race, research suggests they benefit students*. Chalkbeat. https://www.chalkbeat.org/2021/7/8/22569197/critical-race-theory-bans-racism-schools-research

Bell, D. (1992). *Faces at the bottom of the well*. Basic Books.

Benjamin, L. T., Jr. (2009). The birth of American intelligence testing. *American Psychological Association, 40*(1), 20.

Bennett, J. (2020, November 19). What if instead of calling people out, we called them in? Prof. Loretta J. Ross is combating cancel culture with a popular class at Smith College. *New York Times.*

Berry, W. (1970). *The hidden wound.* Houghton Mifflin.

Bonilla-Silva, E. (2009). *Racism without racists: Color-blind racism and the persistence of racial inequality in America* (3rd ed.). Rowman & Littlefield.

Boykin, A. W. & Noguera, P. (2011). *Creating the opportunity to learn: Moving from research to practice to close the achievement gap.* ASCD.

Brosnan, M. & Chandler-Ward, J. (2021, January 27). *Teaching racial truth in America: This year's Black history month is a clarion call.* Teaching While White. https://www.teachingwhilewhite.org/blog/teaching-racial-truth-in-america-this-years-black-history-month-is-a-clarion-call

Bronson, P. & Merryman, A. (2009). *NutureShock: New thinking about children.* Twelve.

Brown, B. (2007). *Thought it was just me.* Gotham Books.

Camera, L. (2021, June 23). Bills banning critical race theory advance in states despite its absence in many classrooms. *US News and World Report.*

Carter, R. & Denevi, E. (2006). Multicultural seminar: A new model for professional development. *Multicultural Perspectives, 8*(2), 18–24.

Chandler-Ward, J. (2016a, March 6). *Rethinking how we choose books in schools.* Teaching While White. https://www.teachingwhilewhite.org/blog/2019/3/6/rethinking-how-we-think-about-choosing-books-in-school

Chandler-Ward, J. (2016b, December 5). *Opening the curtain, closing the gaps between aspiration and reality.* NAIS. https://www.nais.org/learn/independent-ideas/december-2016/opening-the-curtain,-closing-the-gaps-between-aspi/

Chandler-Ward, J. (2017a, May 31). *Your curriculum is already raced.* Teaching While White. https://www.teachingwhilewhite.org/blog/2017/5/31/your-curriculum-is-already-raced

Chandler-Ward, J. (2017b, August 16). *I am Charlottesville.* Teaching While White. https://www.teachingwhilewhite.org/blog/2017/8/16/i-am-charlottesville

Chandler-Ward, J. (2018, March 29). *Teaching English while white.*

Teaching   While   White.   https://www.teachingwhilewhite.org/
blog/2018/3/29/teaching-english-while-white

Chandler-Ward, J. (2019, August 8). *Distancing ourselves from ourselves.*
Teaching   While   White.   https://www.teachingwhilewhite.org/
blog/2019/7/30/distancing-ourselves-from-ourselves

Chandler-Ward, J. & Denevi, E. (2017, April 18). *Foggy mirrors.*
Teaching   While   White.   https://www.teachingwhilewhite.org/
blog/2016/12/27/foggy-mirrors-by-jenna-chandler-ward-elizabeth
-denevi

Chandler-Ward, J. & Denevi, E. (2020, January 28). *White fragility
in students.* The Puzzle Blog. https://www.carneysandoe.com/blog
-post/white-fragility-in-students

Cose, E. (1994). *The rage of a privileged class.* HarperCollins.

Crenshaw, K. (1991). Mapping the margins: Intersectionality, identity politics, and violence against Women of Color. *Stanford Law
Review, 23*(6), 1241–1299.

Delpit, L. (1995). *Other people's children: Cultural conflict in the classroom.* The New Press.

Denevi, E. (2017). What if being called "racist" is the beginning,
not the end, of the conversation? In E. Moore, Jr., A. Michael, &
M. W. Penick-Parks (Eds.), *The guide for white women who teach
Black boys.* Corwin.

Denevi, E. (2004). White on white: Exploring white racial identity,
privilege, and racism. *Independent School, 63*(4), 78–87.

Denevi, E. (2004). Whiteness: Helping white students and educators
understand their role in a multicultural society. *Independent School,
61*(4), 78–87.

Denevi, E. & Richards, M. (2012). *Diversity directors as leaders: Making
the case for excellence.* The Inclusive School, National Association of
Independent Schools.

Denevi, E. & Richards, M. (2012). The necessity of collaborative leadership. *Independent School, 71*(4), 56–61.

Denevi, E. & Pastan, N. (2006). Helping whites develop anti-racist
identities: Overcoming their resistance to fighting racism. *Multicultural Education, 14*(2), 70–73.

Denevi, E. (2004). *Ethnic Voices in Secondary English Education:*

Developing Student and Teacher Understanding through Journal Writing. [Unpublished dissertation, University of London].

DiAngelo, R. (2020). *White fragility: Why it's so hard for white people to talk about racism.* Beacon Press.

Dovidio, J. F. & Gaertner, S. L. (2005, Winter). Color blind or just plain blind?: The pernicious nature of contemporary racism. *The NonProfit Quarterly, 12*(4).

Embrace Race. (2021). *Embrace Race.* https://www.embracerace.org/.

Erakat, N. & Gorski, P. (2019) Racism, whiteness, and burnout in antiracism movements: How white racial justice activists elevate burnout in racial justice activists of color in the United States. *Ethnicities, 19*(5), 784–808

Frankenberg, R. (1993). *White women, race matters: The social construction of whiteness.* University of Minnesota Press.

Gorski, P. (2019). Avoiding racial equity detours. *Educational Leadership, 76*(6).

Gorski, P. & Swalwell, K. (2015, March). Equity literacy for all. *Educational Leadership, 72*(6), 34–40.

Green, E. L. & Waldman, A. (2018, October 16). You are Still Black: Charlottesville Racial Divide Hinders Students. *New York Times.*

Gurin, P., Dey, E., Hurtado, S., & Gurin, G. (2002). Diversity and Higher Education: Theory and Impact on Educational Outcomes. *Harvard Educational Review, 72*(3), 330–367.

Hammond, Z. L. (2015). Culturally responsive teaching and the brain: Promoting authentic engagement and rigor among culturally and linguistically diverse students. Corwin.

Hardiman, R., & Jackson, B. W. (1997). Conceptual foundations for social justice courses. In M. Adams, L. Bell, & P. Griffin (Eds.), *Teaching for diversity and social justice: A sourcebook* (pp. 16–29). Routledge.

Helms, J. (2019). A race is a nice thing to have: A guide to being a white person or understanding the white persons in your life (3rd ed.). Cognella Academic Publishing.

Higgins, M. (2019, Summer). Getting on the Right Track: How One School Stopped Tracking Students. *Learning for Justice, 62.*

hooks, b. (2018). *All about love: New visions* (765th ed.). William Morrow.

Integrated Schools. (2021). *Integrated schools: Families choosing integration.* https://integratedschools.org/

Irving, D. (2014). *Waking up white: And finding myself in the story of race.* Elephant Room Press.

Joffe-Walt, C. (Host). (2020). Nice White Parents (No. 05) [Audio podcast episode].

Kelly, D. J., Quinn, P. C., Slater, A. M., Lee, K., Gibson, A., Smith, M., Ge, L., & Pascalis, O. (2005). Three-month-olds, but not newborns, prefer own-race faces. *Developmental Science, 8*(6), F31–F36.

Kennedy, D. (2021, April 17). Dad who wrote scathing letter to Brearley about race focus: "Someone had to." *New York Post.*

King, J. (2016, May 15). The invisible tax on Teachers of Color. *Washington Post.*

Kivel, P. (2011, September 27). Uprooting racism: How white people can work for racial justice (3rd ed.). New Society Publishers.

Kwon, R. O. (2017, February 20). *34 Books by Women of Color to Read This Year.* Electric Lit. https://electricliterature.com/34-books-by -women-of-color-to-read-this-year/

Lee, E., Menkart, D., & Okazawa-Rey, M. (Eds.). (1998). *Beyond heroes and holidays: A practical guide to K-12 anti-racist, multicultural education and staff development.* Network of Educators on the Americas.

Lewis, A. E. & Diamond, J. B. (2015). *Despite the best intentions: How racial inequality thrives in good schools.* Oxford University Press.

Virginia Museum of History & Culture. (2021). *Massive resistance.* from https://virginiahistory.org/learn/historical-book/chapter/mas sive-resistance

Mathis, W. (May 30, 2013). Research overwhemingly counsels an end to tracking. National Education Policy Center. (https://nepc .colorado.edu/newsletter/2013/05/options-tracking

McGhee, H. (2021). *The sum of us: How racism costs everyone and how we can prosper together.* One World.

McIntyre, A. (1997). *Making meaning of whiteness: Exploring racial identity with white teachers.* State University of New York Press.

McLaren, P. (2014). *Life in Schools* (6th ed.). Paradigm Press.

Michael, A. & Bartoli, E. (2014). *What white children need to know about race.* National Association of Independent Schools. https://

www.nais.org/magazine/independent-school/summer-2014/what
-white-children-need-to-know-about-race/

Moyer, M. (June 25, 2020). What white parents get wrong about raising antiracist kids—and how to get it right. *Washington Post.* https://www.washingtonpost.com/lifestyle/2020/06/25/what-white
-parents-get-wrong-about-raising-antiracist-kids-how-get-it-right/

Noah, T. (2019, February 27). Telling uncomfortable stories (Season 24, Episode 72) [TV Series]. In *The Daily Show with Trevor Noah.*

Oakes, J. (2005). *Keeping track: How schools structure inequality.* Yale University Press.

Okun, T. O. (2020). White Supremacy Culture. Retrieved from https://www.whitesupremacyculture.info/

Page, S. (2008). *Difference: How the power of diversity creates better groups, firms, schools, and societies.* Princeton University Press.

Papageorge, N. W., Gershenson, S., & Min Kang, K. (2020). Teacher Expectations Matter. *The Review of Economics and Statistics, 102*(2), 234–251.

Piazza, P. (2021, February 17). *New research: Benefits for white students in integrated schools.* Integrated Schools. https://sdnotebook.com/2021/02/17/new-research-benefits-for-white-students-in
-integrated-schools/

Pirtle, W. (2019, April 23). The other segregation. *The Atlantic.*

Policy and Program Studies Service Office of Planning, Evaluation, and Policy Development. (2016, July). *The state of racial diversity in the educator workforce.* U.S. Department of Education.

Project Implicit. (2011). *Implicit association test.* Harvard University.

Reardon, S. F., Kalogrides, D., & Shores, K. (2019). The Geography of Racial/Ethnic Test Score Gaps. *The American Journal of Sociology, 124*(4).

Saad, L. (2020). *Me and white supremacy.* Sourcebooks.

Saxman, C. & Tochluk, S. (2020, April 14). *Inoculating our students against white nationalism.* Teaching While White.

Starck, J. G., Riddle, T., Sinclair, S., & Warikoo, N. (2020). Teachers are people Too: Examining the racial bias of teachers compared to other American adults. *Educational Researcher, 49*(4), 273–284.

Steele, C. (2011). *Whistling Vivaldi: How stereotypes affect us and what we can do*. W. W. Norton & Company.

Stevenson, H. C. (2014). *Promoting racial literacy in schools: Differences that make a difference*. Teachers College Press.

Strauss, V. (2019, May 16). Why school integration works. *Washington Post*.

Stuart Wells, A., Fox, L., & Cordova-Cobo, D. (2016, February 9). How racially diverse students and classrooms can benefit all students. *The Century Foundation*.

Sue, D. W., Capodilupo, C. M., Torino, G. C., Bucceri, J. M., Holder, A. M. B., Nadal, K. L., and Esquilin, M. (2007, May–June). Racial Microaggressions in Everyday Life Implications for Clinical Practice. *American Psychologist, 62*(4), 271–286. https://doi.org/10.1037/0003-066X.62.4.271

Tatum, B. D. (1992). Talking about race, learning about racism: The application of racial identity development theory in the classroom. *Harvard Educational Review, 62*(1), 1–24.

Tatum, B. D. (2017). *Why are all the black kids sitting together in the cafeteria?: And other conversations about race*. Basic Books.

The President's Advisory 1776 Commission Report. (2021 January). https://trumpwhitehouse.archives.gov/wp-content/uploads/2021/01/The-Presidents-Advisory-1776-Commission-Final-Report.pdf

Tippett, K. (2020, October 29). The long view, I: On being white: An interview with John Biewen [Audio]. *On Being*. https://onbeing.org/programs/john-biewen-the-long-view-i-on-being-white/

Tippett, K. (2020, July 9). Towards a Framework for Repair: An interview with Robin DiAngelo and Resmaa Menakem [Audio]. *On Being.*https://onbeing.org/programs/robin-diangelo-and-resmaa-menakem-towards-a-framework-for-repair/

Tippett, K. (2013, March 28). Love in Action: am interview with John Lewis [Audio]. *On Being*. https://onbeing.org/programs/john-lewis-love-in-action/

Tochluk, S., & Saxman, C. (2020, April 14). Inoculating Our Students Against White Nationalism. Teaching While White. https://www

.teachingwhilewhite.org/blog/2020/4/13/inoculating-our-students
-against-white-nationalism

Tochluk, S., & Saxman, C. (2019, March 15). Swastikas in the bathroom: connecting the dots between white supremacy, white nationalism, the alt-right, and the alt-light. *Shelly Tochluk*. https://shellytochluk .medium.com/swastikas-in-the-bathroom-connecting-the-dots -between-white-supremacy-white-nationalism-the-dc5d6ec266f2

Tochluk, S. (2010). *Witnessing whiteness: The need to talk about race and how to do it*. Rowman & Littlefield Education.

Turner, C. (2019, October 8) Why All Parents Should Talk to Their Kids About Social Identity. [Audio]. National Public Radio. https:// www.npr.org/2019/10/08/767205198/the-things-parents-dont-talk -about-with-their-kids-but-should

Vatterott, C. (2018). Rethinking homework: Best practices that support diverse needs. ASCD.

Washington, J. "Reframing Resistance to Achieve Cultural Change." Magna Online Seminars.

Weinberg, M. (1975). The relationship between school desegregation and academic achievement: A review of the research. *Law and Contemporary Problems, 39*(2).

Yepes-Amaya, W. (2019, December 19) Equity Audit. University of Massachusetts, Boston.

Yuval-Davis, N. (1997). Women, ethnicity, and empowerment: Towards transversal politics. *Gender and Nation*. Sage.

INDEX

Note: Pages in *italics* refer to figures.

Grading for Equity (Feldman), 105
Grimké, A. E., 159
Grimké, S. M., 159
guilt, 51, 63, 71, 112, 133
  disintegration status in institutions
    and, 34
  no longer being paralyzed by, 27
  racial identity development and,
    16, 24, 25
  see also shame
Gurin, P., 114, 115

Hammond, Z., 84–85, 87, 107
Hampton, F., 156
Harlem Renaissance, 77
Harpers Ferry, West Virginia, slave
    insurrection at, 155
Harris, S., 156
Harvey, J., 139
Hate U Give, The (Thomas), 76
HBCUs. *see* historically Black colleges
    and universities (HBCUs)
Helms, J., xvii, xxii, 15, 16, 24, 25
  institutional statuses and snapshots,
    33–41
  stages of white racial identity
    development, 17–19
"Hidden Wound, The" (Berry), 54
Higgins, M., 145
high-expectation students, prejudice,
    teacher expectations, and, 95
high school students
  racial affinity spaces and, 60, 61
  White Privilege Conference hosted
    by, 67, 151
hiring
  power and, 117
  racial identity development and, 116
  stereotype threat and, 123

historically Black colleges and
    universities (HBCUs), 32
historical truths, racism and erasure
    of, 4
Hitler, A., 163, 164
homework assignments, comments
    for white students *vs.* Students of
    Color, 103–4
honors/AP classes, power and
    enrollment in, 116
hooks, b., 13
Horowitz, R., 159–60
House Un-American Activities
    Committee, 155
"How Can I Have a Positive Racial
    Identity? I'm White" (Michael),
    9
humility
  cultivating, in affinity groups, 58
  value of, xxvii–xxviii
Hurston, Z. N., 77

identification and data, naming
    racism and, 114, 117
identity threat, stress responses tied
    to, 107
identity webs, 62
"if only" statements, white talk and,
    48
"I Have a Dream" speech (King, Jr.),
    164
immersion/emersion stage or status
  Elizabeth's story about navigating,
    25–26
  in Helms's white racial identity
    development model, 19
  institutional demonstration of,
    38–39
  Jenna's story about navigating, 23

ABOUT THE AUTHORS

Jenna Chandler-Ward is the cofounder of the blog and podcast series, Teaching While White. She has been an educator in nonprofits, schools, and colleges for over 20 years, working with students from kindergarten to college level. Most recently, Jenna had been a middle school English and drama teacher outside of Boston. Jenna is also a founder of the Multicultural Teaching Institute, which produces workshops and a conference for educators on issues of identity in education. Jenna currently is an education consultant focusing on whiteness, and lives in Cambridge, MA, on the Ancestral and Traditional land of the Massa-dchu-es-et and the Wampanoag.

As director of East Ed, **Dr. Elizabeth Denevi** works with institutions and schools nationally to increase equity, promote diversity pedagogy, and implement strategic processes for growth and development. She is the cofounder of Teaching While White, a blog and podcast series that promotes antiracist teaching practices. She also serves as an assistant professor at Lewis & Clark College in the Graduate School of Education and Counseling. She has been a classroom teacher and building administrator in a number of K–12 schools and currently lives in Oregon on the Ancestral and Traditional lands of the Chinook.